The 125 Most-Asked Questions About Cats

(And the Answers)

The 125 Most-Asked Questions About Cats

(And the Answers)

John Malone

William Morrow and Company, Inc., New York

It is the policy of William Morrow and Company, Inc., and its imprints and affiliates, recognizing the importance of preserving what has been written, to print the books we publish on acid-free paper, and we exert our best efforts to that end.

Library of Congress Cataloging-in-Publication Data

Malone, John Williams.
    The 125 most-asked questions about cats (and the answers) / by John Malone.
        p. cm.
    Includes bibliographical references and index.
    ISBN 0-688-10552-1
    1. Cats—Miscellanea.   I. Title.   Title: One hundred twenty-five most-asked questions about cats.
SF442.M315   1992
636.8—dc20   91-36128
                                                                    CIP

Printed in the United States of America

First Edition

1 2 3 4 5 6 7 8 9 10

BOOK DESIGN AND ILLUSTRATIONS BY KARIN BATTEN

Contents

The 125 Most-Asked Questions About Cats

(And the Answers)

1
Hieroglyphic Cats

Q. I know domestic cats aren't directly descended from large cats like lions and tigers but from a related yet separate line, just as human beings don't come directly from apes. But I hear a lot of different things about where the first domestic cats appeared. *Are domestic cats descended from a smallish African or European wild cat?*

A. There has been a great deal of controversy about this for a long time. Modern domestic cats look more like the wild European cat known as *Felis silvestris* (yes, that's where Sylvester the cartoon cat got his name), but many experts are convinced that the African cat *F. libyca* is the more likely line. For one thing, it has been found that when a wild *F. libyca* is mated to a domestic cat, the resulting offspring can be tamed, which is not the case with the offspring of a domestic cat and *F. silvestris*. Some experts don't accept this evi-

13

dence, however, and insist that the *libyca* is just a variation of the *silvestris*.

Whatever the genetic truth, there is no argument concerning the first records of domestic cats. The earliest pictorial representations date to Egyptian paintings as far back as 2600 B.C. These still might have been wild cats, however. Skeletons of cats, with small eating bowls beside them, were found in a tomb dating to 1900 B.C., by which time they were clearly household animals. And as of 1600 B.C., the records become numerous, not only in paintings and sculpture but also in hieroglyphic references. From 1000 B.C. until the early years of the Christian era, cats were sacred in Egypt, worshipped as embodiments of the goddess known as Pash, Bast, or Bastet. Some linguists in fact believe that the word "puss" comes from the name Pash.

2

Geographical Hash

Q. There are so many cat breeds, like Siamese and Abyssinian and Burmese, with names that seem to indicate that these breeds originally came from particular regions of the world, but I know that some of these names are misleading. *Is there any rule of thumb used to name breeds according to geographical origin?*

A. It is about as fruitless to attempt to make a connection between actual places and the names of cat breeds as it is to seek hidden messages in a bowl of alphabet soup. There are a few connections that make sense: The Siamese probably did originate in Siam (now Thailand) and the Maine coon did develop in New England, probably as a cross between an indigenous breed and the cats brought there by early settlers. But the Havana brown is named for its cigarlike color and was bred in England, not Cuba. The Himalayan has nothing to do with Tibet or *Lost Horizon,* and the Persian could just as easily be connected to Russia or Afghanistan or even China. The naming of cat breeds has far more to do with human fancy than it does with geographical origin.

3

The Cat That Walks by Himself

🐾

Q. People are always talking about how independent, even aloof, cats are. I have a cat named Kate and a dog named Spencer who are practically inseparable, and have been since they were only a few weeks old. *Is it really true that dogs are social animals and cats are not?*

A. Your situation is a special one, although it is by no means rare. Cats and dogs can become fast friends when introduced at a young enough age. This can also happen, though less commonly, when there is a considerable age difference between them. But it is more usual for cats and dogs in the same household to simply tolerate one another. At any rate, the fact that a pet cat and dog get along is not really evidence of the degree to which they are social animals.

Part of the problem here is semantic. Zoologists classify animals as social or not according to the kind of society they create for themselves in the wild. Do they form packs? Do they hunt cooperatively? Wild dogs do. Wild cats, with the exception of the lion, do not. A wild cat "walks by himself," in Kipling's phrase, and hunts by himself—or herself.

It should be noted that this is an area in which there is disagreement among experts. A distinct minority claims that cats in the wild, despite the fact that they don't hunt cooperatively, do have a hierarchy of dominance. This may be true to an extent, but that still does not involve cooperation, and cooperation is the crux of the matter. Females will sometimes nurse one another's kittens, but they will also steal them, which is hardly cooperative.

Further confusion arises from the fact that kittens are spoken of as becoming "socialized" during the period they play with one another. But becoming socialized is a matter of learning to relate to another animal (and eventually to human beings); it is not the same thing as forming a cooperative social group, which is another step entirely.

4

Cat Haters

Q. I had an extraordinary thing happen to me recently. A man who had been a friend for several years refused to come to my apartment anymore because I had adopted a cat owned by a friend who had been posted overseas. The first time he walked in and saw the cat, he turned deathly pale, started to shake all over, turned heel, and fled. Later I asked him if he was allergic. He said he didn't know because he didn't stay around cats long enough to find out. He simply hated them. I can understand someone being afraid of dogs if he or she had a bad experience as a child. *But why would anyone hate cats so much that he or she can't stand to be in the same room with them?*

A. A given individual may have a special problem relating to cats without fully understanding it, based on a repressed childhood memory of some sort. But ailurophobia, as cat hating or fearing is called, is not uncommon. The Greeks had a very ambivalent attitude toward cats, perhaps because the Egyptians worshipped them. Julius Caesar and both Henri II and Charles XI of France are reported to have nearly fainted whenever a cat came near them. It is known that Napoleon hated cats and broke out in a sweat in their presence (this could have been an allergic reaction).

Mass cat hating was the rule from the 1300s to the late 1700s across Europe and in many of the American colonies. But this epidemic of ailurophobia was the result of the association of cats with witches. This idea was backed up by actual papal decree and was picked up even by the Puritan Protestant sects. Cats, and their suspect owners, were routinely tortured, splayed, and burned. Even Elizabeth I had a penchant

18

for burning cats. The cat regained respectability toward the end of the seventeenth century, largely because of its ability to catch rats, which had virtually overrun many urban centers. But four centuries of mass hatred of cats undoubtedly left its mark—the residual loathing still crops up today, sometimes in surprising people.

5

Crossed Paths

Q. I just got a beautiful Bombay kitten that's almost as black and shiny as patent leather. Not having had a black cat before, I am amazed to discover how many people believe their lives will go to wrack and ruin if a black cat crosses their path. *Is the fear of black cats simply a holdover from old nonsense about their being the familiars of witches?*

A. No doubt that is part of it, but the superstition about black cats is a peculiarly American one. It may have something to do with Halloween, which we make so much of, but it's difficult to be sure. And in both Asia and England black cats are considered lucky.

6

Fancy That Cat

Q. The Cat Fanciers Association seems an excellent name for an organization devoted to the love of cats and the celebration of the various breeds. But I don't entirely understand the use of the term the "cat fancy." *Where does the term the "cat fancy" come from?*

A. The "cat fancy" is a curious term. It refers to anything and everything about breeding, owning, and loving cats. It has its roots in the tremendous new interest in cats that arose in England during the last two decades of the nineteenth century. While the exact derivation is obscure, it clearly draws upon two different meanings of the word "fancy" in Great Britain. On the more obvious level it has to do with fancy cats—that is, purebred cats. But the British also speak of "fancying" things, anything from a scarf to a painting to a person. This suggestion of liking something a lot and wishing to possess it is also part of the meaning of the cat fancy.

7

From the Crystal Palace to Madison Square Garden

🐾

Q. I enjoy going to both dog shows and cat shows simply because of the beauty of the animals. But a cat show sometimes seems like a Miss America Pageant with the talent competition left out. I understand that dog shows got their start as competitions among working dogs in rural areas. *Who came up with the idea for the first cat show?*

A. A British cat enthusiast named Harrison Weir organized the first cat show in 1871 at the famed Crystal Palace, originally erected in London's Hyde Park in 1851 for the Great Exhibition and then moved to Sydenham on the outskirts of London. The first major cat show in the United States was held ten years later on lower Broadway in New York City at the museum of G. B. Bunnell, who had copied P. T. Barnum's idea of an exhibition hall that combined edification with entertainment.

While it is true that cats are not required to demonstrate their training in the way that show dogs must, cat shows are extremely popular; upwards of seventy-five thousand purebred cats are judged at more than three hundred shows in the United States every year. The largest is New York's International Cat Show held at Madison Square Garden.

8

Breed Categories

🐾

Q. I have a wonderful Burmese cat named Mandalay. I have been told that Burmese cats are an established breed. Yet I'm certain that Burmese cats were developed by a long process of selective breeding. It seems to me they ought to be in the hybrid category. *What exactly are the criteria by which breeds of cat are assigned to particular categories?*

A. This is an area fraught with confusion and debate. Let's start with what are called natural breeds. These are cats that are believed to have developed on their own without human intervention. The Egyptian Mau, the Abyssinian, the Japanese bobtail, the Siamese, the American shorthair, the Turkish angora, the Maine coon, and the Manx are all usually regarded as natural breeds. But there are some problems even here. The American shorthair undoubtedly developed on its own, but the common American shorthair, of which there are millions, would not be allowed to participate in a cat show (except in the informal house pet categories). To be eligible, an American shorthair must have pedigree papers, which means that human intervention has indeed taken place. This is called bringing the breed "up to standard," but that in itself tends to contravene the word "natural." The official rationale here is that the word "natural," in this context, means mating cats of the same breed to one another, as in a Japanese bobtail to a Japanese bobtail. The terminology does confuse the layperson.

The second category to consider is that of hybrid breeds. In this case, two or more natural breeds are mated to produce a new breed such as the Himalayan, the cross between the Siamese and the Persian. But a given breed of cat does not necessarily stay in the hybrid category. After it has been around long enough, and it has been found that the mating of two cats of the same hybrid breed produces offspring that remain true to the new form, the breed will eventually be moved into the established breed category. This is what happened with the Burmese cat. Once a breed has been declared established, cats of that breed are no longer allowed to be produced through crossbreeding, at least for show purposes. The Balinese, the Birman, and the Havana brown are other cats that have been placed in the established breed category.

9

Cracking the Social Register

Q. I have a beautiful cat of the Oriental longhair breed, a relatively new variety. It was recognized as a breed by The International Cat Association in 1984. Finally, the Cat Fanciers Association recognized it in 1988, but it still isn't allowed to be entered in competition by the CFA. *Why do TICA and the CFA have different criteria when deciding whether or not to admit a new breed to competition?*

A. Because the two organizations are themselves in competition. The CFA considers TICA to be too quick to give accreditation; TICA considers the CFA too conservative. The cat fancier will have to use his or her own judgment concerning this argument, but it may be helpful to view the matter in the same light as the American League/National League difference of opinion about the use of the designated hitter in baseball, or the endless disputes between boxing organizations about who should be declared World Champion in various weight divisions. Such debates always seem to involve more than meets the eye.

10

Pedigree Accuracy

🐾

Q. My Maine coon has a pedigree that goes back eight generations and lists a champion in the sixth generation. *How can I be certain this is accurate information and does it affect the judging at a cat show?*

A. You can't be certain of the accuracy of a pedigree, not because anyone is necessarily being dishonest but rather because slipups do occur in this complicated kind of record keeping. You need the pedigree papers to enter your cat in a show, but judges pay attention only to the cat in front of them at the given moment. After all, there are "black sheep" in every bloodline as well as "commoners" that rise to fame.

11

Ordinary Show-offs

Q. I have no pedigree papers for my cat, but he is a very handsome creature with long silky red and white hair. *Are there shows at which nonpurebred cats can compete against one another?*

A. Many localities across the country have informal cat shows at which cats of any status may be shown. Even some of the larger official cat shows have special categories for cats that are other than purebred, although most of these are limited to cats of new breeds that have not yet been accepted for competition. This gives the breeders and owners of new strains of cats an opportunity to display their cats and try to persuade the powers that be that the time has come for full certification.

12

A Rainbow of Colors

Q. I went to my first cat show last week. I was astonished by the extraordinary number of colors among the cats on view. But when the cats were being judged, I noticed that some breeds come in very few colors, and others in what seems like dozens. *Why are some breeds of cats considered purebred in such a narrow range of color and others in such a broad one?*

A. There is no simple answer to this question, since the rules have been evolving for more than a hundred years. It should be understood, however, that even when the range of colors is very broad (there are thirty-three possibilities for American shorthairs, for example) the way the colors are distributed within a particular color range to form a pattern are much narrower than it might seem. The ideal is sufficiently spelled out for a judge to quickly spot a flaw even in particolored cats like the tortoiseshell.

Coloration is divided into two main categories by the CFA: Spectrum A and Spectrum B. Spectrum A is very broad, but broken down into five subcategories: solid colors, shaded, smoke, tabbies, and particolors. Each of these subcategories is further subdivided; under smoke, for instance, there are black, blue, and red divisions. Spectrum B is very narrow, describing only four color combinations: seal point, chocolate point, blue point, and lilac point. In each case there is a basic body color and a contrasting color at the points (head, feet, and tail). The quintessential Spectrum B cat is the Siamese.

13

Like Watered Silk

🐾

Q. I thought that "tabby" was a generic name for any kind of cat, but I recently learned that it is a specific category of cat. *How many varieties of tabby are there and where does the name come from?*

A. "Tabby" refers to markings rather than color or specific breed. There is a chocolate tabby angora, a blue classic tabby Persian, and even a Siamese called chocolate-lynx point colorpoint. Maine coons often have tabby markings in a wide variety of color combinations. The striped-and-barred tabby pattern derives its name from a quarter of old Baghdad called Attibya, which was famous for its production of watered silk with a characteristic wavy appearance.

14

Furbelows of Fur Balls

Q. I took my seven-year-old daughter to a local cat show. She was enthralled and wants a cat badly. The problem is that she will not settle for anything but a Persian. *Don't Persian cats require more care than just about any other breed?*

A. Persian cats certainly require more grooming than any other kinds of cats. The wonderful furbelow, or ruff, of hair around the neck, as well as the length of the hair all over the body, creates hair balls of epic dimensions that can be dangerous to the cat since they are difficult to disgorge. Thus the owner of these regal creatures must be prepared to brush them at least once a day and preferably twice. The procedure takes time; it must be done carefully because the Persian's fur tends to come out in tufts and can leave bald spots. What's more, many Persians do not like to be brushed. You have to insist.

Despite this extra work, Persians are the second most popular cats to Siamese. A great many people think their beauty and calm disposition are well worth the effort. I've known several children as young as your daughter who have taken on this task with great devotion, and there's no doubt that the child who must care for a Persian learns fine lessons about responsibility. Make sure your daughter understands what her duties will be beforehand, and there's no reason the situation can't benefit both child and cat.

15

Rare As Tortoiseshell

Q. I recently admired a friend's tortoiseshell Persian cat and thought I would like to have one myself. When she told me how much it cost, I nearly passed out and dropped the subject. *Why are cats with a tortoiseshell pattern so expensive?*

A. Purebred tortoiseshells are extremely difficult to breed. The markings are due to a lack of an X chromosome. Thus a tortoiseshell cat is a female more than 990 times out of 1,000 and the very few males that are born are almost invariably sterile. A breeder is thus starting from scratch, as it were, every time, using either two nontortoiseshell cats of the same breed that might result in the desired markings, or breeding a nontortoiseshell male to a tortoiseshell female, which is scarcely less frustrating. The difficulty involved inevitably increases the price.

16

A Green-Eyed Gaze

Q. I want to get my wife a cat for her birthday. She has green eyes and it would be nice to get a cat that's also green-eyed. *Are there breeds of cats that you can count on to have green eyes?*

A. Your best chances of acquiring a green-eyed cat lie with three of the lesser-known breeds. The Korat, which is not very common even in its native Thailand, is a silver-blue cat with exceptionally large green or greenish-gold eyes. And it is difficult to know how green its eyes will be when a Korat is a kitten; at that point they are usually amber. Another possibility, the Egyptian Mau, is interesting in that it is the only true spotted cat among the domestic breeds, with the spots overlaid on a basic coat of silver, bronze, or smoke. The eyes are usually light green but are sometimes amber. Your best bet may be the Havana brown, a cat growing in popularity. It doesn't come from Cuba—the "Havana" refers to the cigar color. An elegant and unusual cat, the Havana brown purebred should always have chartreuse green eyes. There are some other far more common breeds, like the Maine coon, that sometimes have green eyes, but the eye color may not be fixed in a kitten.

17

Rumpy and Stumpy

Q. An acquaintance of mine has a Manx that has a tail of almost regular length. She insists it is a purebred cat, but I find that hard to believe. I've heard of Manx cats having some tail, but not a regulation one. *Isn't it true that a genuine Manx should really be tailless?*

A. The Manx, named for the Isle of Man where it was developed—probably from a tailless Asian cat—is unusual in its genetic pattern. Most modern breeds that have been developed depend upon recessive genes for their special characteristics, which is why breeding them is often frustrating and difficult. The gene that is of importance for the missing tail of the Manx is, however, a dominant gene. But it does not always dominate completely. Thus two purebred Manxes, both tailless, can produce a litter that contains tailless kittens, kittens with partial tails, and the occasional kitten with a tail of almost "normal" length. Tailless Manxes are called "rumpies"; those with a partial tail are called "stumpies." Only those without any tail are accepted for cat show purposes.

18

Matchless Marmalades

Q. I am confused about marmalade cats. I think they're beautiful but a lot of them seem to be alley cats. *Is there such a thing as a purebred marmalade cat?*

A. There is no breed called marmalade. Marmalade coloration, however, is found in several breeds, including Persian and Siamese. The striped marmalade alley cat configuration is one of the many colorations of both American and British shorthairs. You can tell a purebred not only by the fine quality of its coat but also by the fact that the markings will be symmetrical on both sides.

19

The Everest of Breeding

Q. It seems as though new breeds of cats are being introduced every few years. *What cat breed is regarded as the most
successful new development in the past half century?*

A. That honor certainly belongs to the Himalayan for two
reasons. First, it required an enormous amount of trial and
error to perfect this cross between the Siamese and the Persian breeds. The Himalayan draws upon the coloring of the
Siamese and the long hair and body shape of the Persian. Second, this spectacularly beautiful cat, which comes in an aston-
ishing range of colors, has achieved a popularity exceeded
only by that of the two breeds from which it was created.

20

Crossed Eyes and Kinky Tails

Q. I've been offered a five-month-old Siamese cat. The owner has several purebred Siamese cats which she enters in cat shows, and they've won a number of prizes. This cat has a kinky tail and slightly crossed eyes, and apparently that makes it unacceptable as a show cat. My friend says it is also a purebred, and that Siamese cats often have these problems. *Why do some Siamese cats have kinky tails and crossed eyes, and does that mean there's something else more seriously wrong with them?*

A. Kinky tails are a recurring problem for breeders of Siamese cats. The kink is a sign of their Asian ancestry; many cats in the Far East have kinky tails. As for the crossed eyes, that too is a genetic problem, connected to the albino genes that give Siamese their special colorations. Muriel Beadle provides a very detailed scientific explanation of this condition in her book, *The Cat.* To put it simply, all Siamese cats have an excess of retinal nerves that cross over from one brain hemisphere to the other, where they get "wired" wrong. This would give the cat double vision if it could not compensate. Some Siamese compensate by "repressing" one set of nerve messages. Other cats manage to reroute the conflicting messages. Those that repress the extra message have normal-appearing eyes and are thus eligible for show competition. But those that reroute the messages develop crossed eyes as they mature and cannot be entered in a show.

Neither the kinky tail nor the crossed eyes are indicative of any other problem, and cats with these attributes still make splendid pets.

21

Too Many Toes

Q. I recently moved from Minnesota to western Massachusetts. I'm struck by how many cats there are in this area with six toes on their forefeet. *Are six-toed cats a deformity that just happens to crop up more in certain kinds of cats, or is this a mutation that is passed on from generation to generation?*

A. Usually, this is considered a deformity. There are some breeds of cats, the Russian blue, for example, that are more prone to be six-toed than others. In the case of a Russian blue, extra toes would make the cat ineligible for show. However, in the area you live in, six-toed cats have become so common that some experts look upon this feature as an established mutation. It is believed that this mutation first became common in Boston, but it has spread to several surrounding states. These cats are not considered a separate breed, however, since their markings, colorings, and other distinguishing features vary too widely for such a classification.

22

Blue-Eyed and Deaf?

Q. A friend promised my daughter the pick of the litter her cat just had. My daughter is enthralled with a white kitten with blue eyes, and this worries me. *Aren't all white cats with blue eyes deaf?*

Q. The belief that white cats with blue eyes are always deaf goes back a long way. The extent to which the idea was accepted is attested to by a line from Alfred, Lord Tennyson's poem "Lancelot and Elaine": "I will be deaf as a blue-eyed cat." But in fact not all white blue-eyed cats suffer from hearing loss. It's a matter of genetics. If the cat has two genes for whiteness, the chances are quite high that it will be deaf, since the double white genes often result in a deformity of the inner ear. But it doesn't always happen; sometimes another gene offsets the potential deformity. White cats with one blue eye and one yellow one are much less likely to be deaf.

The reason that white cats with blue eyes continue to exist is that people like your daughter find them beautiful. Otherwise this vulnerable strain would have died out long ago. A deaf cat can still be a loving pet, but it must always be kept indoors; outside on its own it would be thoroughly defenseless.

23

Lonely Cats

Q. I'm single and often work long hours. I would like to get a cat, but I worry about leaving it alone a lot. *Are there cats that do better on their own for long days, and what breeds should be avoided by a busy single person?*

A. There are a number of breeds you should definitely avoid. Siamese cats can deal with a standard nine-to-five situation, but people who put in a lot of overtime should think again about a Siamese; it's a very talkative breed and it doesn't like to converse with the furniture. Persians are even more dependent on human company. But the most possessive of all breeds is probably the Burmese. They are wonderful creatures but those who have them often make remarks like "I am owned by a Burmese." Burmese simply hate to be left alone and will even develop psychosomatic illnesses if they don't have enough company.

The American shorthair, the Maine coon, and the Manx are all of a sufficiently independent nature to do better by themselves. The Maine coon, however, is a very large cat and likes space; it's not a cat for a small, two-room apartment.

24
Female Only

:

Q. I own a female tortoiseshell Persian. I would like to mate her, but I am aware that Persians with these markings are always female. *What kinds of kittens am I likely to get if I mate my female tortoiseshell Persian with a male tortoiseshell of another breed?*

A. If you are expecting to get tortoiseshell kittens, you had better contact a recognized cattery that specializes in the tortoiseshell Persian. Producing these purebreds is a very tricky business. If you don't care about the coloration of the kittens, you can be sure of one thing no matter what the breed of the father is: The kittens will be well cared for since tortoiseshell Persians are terrific mothers.

Male tortoiseshell Persians do exist, by the way, but they are very rare—only about one out of three thousand—and they are invariably sterile.

25

Male or Female Preferred

Q. I am on the verge of getting a cat. Some friends tell me that female cats make better pets, others insist it's males. *Is there any real evidence that one sex or the other is a more successful house cat?*

A. This is really a matter of personal preference or, more to the point, prejudice. Provided your cat is going to be neutered, it really doesn't make that much difference. Male cats are more prone to certain kinds of medical problems, females to others, but it's still a toss-up. The same is true in terms of personality: There are aggressive females and docile males. Choose the kitten that most appeals to you and don't worry about its sex.

26

A Sweet Disposition

Q. Our household consists of my husband and myself, two young children, and my mother, who is somewhat frail. I want a cat that is above all good-natured. *Are there certain breeds that are more noted for their sweet dispositions than others?*

A. Some cat fanciers would say yes to this question, or at least warn you away from certain breeds that are supposedly more difficult. But, as Roz Riddle makes clear in *The City Cat*, it is not so much a matter of different breeds as it is what a cat of any breed has been bred for. Cats that are bred primarily for looks, in order to make them highly competitive at cat shows, can sometimes be more high-strung. But there are also cats of most breeds that are specifically bred for good dispositions. They are as much purebreds as their show-oriented cousins, but a loving nature has been given priority over a perfectly formed head. Purebreds that are selected for their disposition give you a better chance at having a sweetheart of a cat than nonepurebreds or those purebreds that are selected for physical configuration. It isn't that the nonpurebred or "show" cat is unlikely to have a good disposition—many of both kinds are perfect darlings—but a cat that is specifically bred for disposition is your best bet.

27

Give Me a Dulcet Tone

Q. I had cats as a child, but for various reasons I haven't had a pet in years. I would like to get a cat again, and I'm very taken with Siamese cats because they are so lively and affectionate, quite aside from their beauty. The one thing that worries me is that I conduct most of my business out of my house. Siamese seem to be rather noisy cats and I'm afraid I might find that distracting. *Are there any cats that are especially sweet-voiced?*

A. You are right to have some concern about a Siamese cat being a distraction. It is the most popular kind of cat among cat fanciers, but also extremely talkative, and the red point Siamese in particular has a quite piercing voice. You would probably be happier with an Abyssinian. They come in both a ruddy and a red coloring, and like the Siamese they are lively, busy, and affectionate. But they have small, very sweet voices that are often called "bell-like."

28

Getting a Kitten

Q. I want to give my granddaughter a kitten for her ninth birthday. This has been talked over with her parents and they are perfectly agreeable. *Where is the best place to get a kitten?*

A. If you want a pedigreed kitten you need to decide what kind and then go to a recognized breeder in your area. The Cat Fanciers Association publishes a breeders' directory. Pedigreed cats are expensive, however, and it seems beside the point to give a show cat to a child. Many people buy kittens at pet shops—and many regret doing so. There are reputable pet shops, of course, but there are many that pass off animals that are diseased. Your best bet is probably your local animal shelter. It is likely to have a wide variety of kittens to choose from, and many shelters, especially private ones, will give the kitten its shots before you take it home.

But there is another factor to consider here. When giving

kittens (or puppies, for that matter) as birthday presents, people often want to surprise the recipient. This does give a jolt of short-term pleasure, but most cat experts suggest that it is a bad idea. The owner-to-be should be allowed to choose his or her own pet. There is some mysterious chemistry involved in choosing a pet. Parents often find that if they allow their child to make the choice, it is quite different from the one they would have made. It's not just that having the choice gives a greater sense of bonding to the child. Kittens make a choice, too. The same kitten can be observed begging to be chosen by one child and totally ignoring another. Let your granddaughter and the right kitten choose each other.

29

The Socialized Kitten

🐾

Q. I have a six-year-old mixed-breed calico. A friend has offered me a beautiful cream-colored exotic shorthair kitten. *What is the best time to bring a new kitten home if you already have a cat?*

A. Some cats tolerate a new addition to the household better than others, but it's very difficult to tell ahead of time. In terms of the new kitten, however, it's possible to be more specific. A litter of kittens that is kept together becomes more socialized to other cats as the weeks go on. Most kittens enter the phase of greatest interactive play at eleven or twelve weeks. Provided there will be at least one other kitten remaining in the litter that long, it can be beneficial to wait as long as thirteen weeks before bringing your kitten home. It won't make any difference in the attitude of the cat you already have, but it is likely to mean that the kitten will be less timid and better able to develop a relationship with the older cat.

At whatever point you bring the kitten home, it is vital to introduce the old cat and the new kitten slowly. Keep them in separate rooms at first. They will both realize from noises and odor that the other exists. Switch them back and forth in the two rooms on a regular basis so that they can get used to each other's smell. Keep this up for several days at least. When you do put the cats together in the same room, stay with them. Even if things seem to be going well, don't leave the house without putting the cats in separate rooms while you are out. Once the cats have dealt with having the run of the house for several successive days without problems during periods that you are at home, you can assume that the situation has become settled.

30

Vaccinations

Q. I've just acquired a kitten from a friend. Little Domino is going to be strictly an indoor cat. *Is there any need to have an indoor cat vaccinated for rabies, and are there any other shots it should have?*

A. An indoor cat doesn't need to be vaccinated for rabies unless you live in a state that requires it by law. But there are two other shots it is imperative that you have your veterinarian give your cat. The first is for *feline panleukopenia,* which you may hear referred to as cat fever or even distemper, even though it is not related to canine distemper. It is a virus that causes acute gastrointestinal distress; the mortality rate is about 50 percent, with kittens especially at risk. A kitten should be vaccinated by the time it is ten weeks old. It should also have a shot for feline leukemia. This was once the most often fatal disease that affected cats. It is a highly contagious virus; a single infected cat can pass the disease on to an entire household of cats. The virus itself was identified in 1964, but it was not until the mid-1980s that a vaccine was developed. Every cat should have this shot.

Many but not all veterinarians combine the feline distemper shot with vaccines for two upper respiratory viruses, *rhinotracheitis* and *calici.*

31

The Cat and the Baby

Q. I am pregnant with our first child. We have a four-year-old female Siamese who is a very lively creature. *Are there special precautions that need to be taken when a baby is brought home to a house already inhabited by a cat?*

A. Some cat lovers get huffy at the idea that an adorable little cat could be a danger to a baby, but caution is in order. First, a rambunctious cat could scratch an infant without meaning harm, or lie down next to and possibly smother the infant. Second, the infant is an intruder on the cat's territory, and the cat may not like that, no matter how sweet and gentle Tabby may seem to be. At the beginning, your cat should never be allowed in the same room as the baby unless someone else is there. This means a closed door to the infant's room, one that latches securely. I have known people who have installed a screen door with a latch, which makes it easier to hear the baby. How long such precautions are necessary depends on the cat and its particular reactions. Sometimes a cat will almost instantly appoint itself the guardian of the new life in the house, which can be a lovely thing to watch, but even in this situation, it's important to make sure the cat doesn't take to licking the baby as though the baby were her own offspring.

32

Snooting Your Cat

Q. I just got a fifteen-week-old kitten for my daughter, who's eight. It was a Christmas surprise, but it's turning out to be a major problem. The kitten won't have anything to do with my daughter. The more she tries to hold it, the more it resists her. She started chasing the kitten around the house, which I put a quick stop to, but my daughter is still very frustrated, and I'm afraid she's starting to actively dislike the kitten. *What can be done to get a cat that doesn't like to be handled to become a little more cuddly?*

A. Your first mistake was to make the kitten a surprise. As I have already mentioned, a child and a kitten should be allowed to choose each other. But don't lose hope. I went through this myself to some extent with my calico named Zelda (as in Fitzgerald). She would dance away from me the moment I showed any interest in picking her up. So I snooted her, paying absolutely no attention to her aside from feeding her. Within twenty-four hours she was rubbing herself against my leg. I tried to pick her up—and away she danced. So that was the game! From then on, even if she rubbed against me, I paid no attention. Within a few days she was climbing up into my lap. I petted her but did not hold her. In the end, Zelda got so she would sit in my lap while I typed. But if I reached down to pick her up, away she went. She never stopped playing that game.

33

What's in a Name?

Q. A friend of mine, a heretical dog lover, says that cats do not recognize their names as such. Now it's true that my three cats don't necessarily come when they're called, but I swear that they do respond at times to their specific names. *Do cats know their own names?*

A. This is a sticky question, to say the least. Cat lovers, myself included, would like to think that the truth of the matter lies in the lines from T. S. Eliot's "The Naming of Cats" that were used in the Andrew Lloyd Webber musical *Cats:*

> When you notice a cat in profound meditation
> The reason, I tell you, is always the same:
> His mind is engaged in a rapt contemplation
> Of the thought, of the thought, of the thought of his
> name:
> His ineffable, effable
> Effanineffable
> Deep and inscrutable singular Name.

Unfortunately, most experts on cats say it just isn't so. Your cats may indeed sometimes seem to respond individually to their names, but that is quite certainly because you speak to them with slightly different inflections that are too subtle even for you to be aware of. The cats are responding to syllables and the pitch at which they are uttered, not to the word as a particular name. To make all this even more humiliating, dogs do respond to specific names, to the extent that you can confuse a young dog by calling it too many nicknames.

34

A Rare Gait

Q. I know that cats walk in an unusual way, moving both legs on one side forward and then both legs on the other side. *Are there any other animals that walk like a cat?*

A. There are only two other mammals that move both their legs on a single side forward simultaneously, the camel and the giraffe. To the observer, both of these animals appear to have an odd, slightly lurching gait. The reason a cat's stride is so smooth is that its legs are also turned in under its body when it walks. Thus the rear paw comes down in almost the same space as that vacated by the front paw on the same side. Not only does that give a smoothness of movement, it also contributes to the extraordinary balance that makes it possible for a cat to securely negotiate the narrow top of a fence.

35

By a Whisker

Q. Our neighbor's six-year-old son cut off the whiskers on the left side of our cat's face. The boy got thoroughly scratched in the process, so I don't think he'll do it again. But for a day or two, our cat, a three-year-old male named Ernest, seemed a little nervous and disoriented. *How important are a cat's whiskers and exactly what do they do?*

A. Ernest had every right to be nervous and disoriented, because a cat's whiskers are very important. Exactly what they do is something of an open question; they seem to have several possible functions. Until fairly recently it was generally believed, even by experts in animal behavior, that the chief function of the whiskers was to give a cat warning that a space it was trying to get through was too small. I used to think that myself. In the mid-1960s I rented a three hundred-year-old house out in the country on the Spanish island of Ibiza for a few months while the woman who lived there returned to America for a visit. She had a cat named Syrup that I was charged with looking after. Syrup didn't have to be let in and out since the first floor of the ancient farmhouse was packed dirt and there was a hole under one of the double wooden doors that she could crawl under. But then Syrup, a delicate little marmalade tabby, got pregnant. One night I was awakened by a pitiful howling. I rushed downstairs and found her stuck under the door. I assumed the added girth from her pregnancy had outwitted her whiskers, and so I made the hole a little bigger.

In recent years, however, a number of experts have questioned this "measuring the hole" idea, noting that the length of a cat's whiskers don't necessarily correlate with the cat's girth. What's more, whiskers, which are technically called *vibrissae*, don't grow just on a cat's face. These stiff, coarse hairs appear not only on the upper lip and at the back of the cheeks, but also on the backs of the forelegs. Veterinarian and animal behaviorist Dr. Michael W. Fox believes that the whiskers are primarily used to locate the direction of an odor by picking it up from the slightest air current. He also notes that if you touch a cat's whiskers, it will almost instantaneously close its eyes. Thus they may be protective in this sense. Other experts, while granting that the vibrissae do serve as a sort of smelling radar, insist that they also play a part in measuring spaces.

Experiments have shown that kittens are not much affected when their whiskers are cut. But mature cats, like your Ernest, do sometimes become temporarily disoriented. They quickly learn to compensate with their other senses, however, and the whiskers will grow back.

36

Purring for What?

Q. The other day I heard my cat purring rather loudly on the back porch. It was a mild spring day and the sun was warming the porch nicely. My thought was that Blossom was in an especially happy mood. But the purring continued in an oddly insistent way, and when I looked out, I discovered that Blossom was in fact in distress. Her hind legs were covered with burrs and she had bloodied her nose trying to get them off. *What causes a cat to purr and why would one purr in distress?*

A. It is believed that the purring sound is made by two folds in the larynx lying behind the true vocal chords. Some experts contend that the purr is a behavior left over from infancy. Kittens first begin to purr when they are nursing. But is it primarily a sound of contentment or an expression of need? It usually seems to indicate contentment, but as in the case of your Blossom, it can also clearly indicate a need for help. Even dying cats have been known to purr.

An even greater mystery is why kittens do not choke on the mother's milk while they are purring. How is it possible to swallow and breathe in and out to activate the purr at the same time? No one really knows.

37

Vocalese

Q. I have two cats, a Siamese and an American shorthair. It seems to me that the Siamese not only "talks" a lot more than the shorthair but also makes a greater variety of sounds. *How many different sounds can cats make and is there a difference between breeds?*

A. Most of what is written about the vocal sounds of cats goes back to a single scientific study made by Mildred Moelk in 1944. According to her study, cats have sixteen different sounds in their repertoire. These are divided into three groups: murmur patterns, which are essentially purring sounds; vowel patterns, which are variations on "meow" sounds; and strained intensity sounds including the hiss and the scream. As a writer, I find the very term "strained intensity" strained, the kind of jargon scientists in many fields resort to when they're having trouble making exact distinctions. Be that as it may, this is an area in desperate need of further research. I would join you and many other cat lovers in suspecting that different breeds have larger or smaller "vocabularies," with the Siamese right up there at the top.

38

Tell-Tail

Q. I have several cats and one of the many fascinations of watching them is the variety of tail movements they make. *To what extent do cats have a readable tail "vocabulary"?*

A. Most experts believe it is very readable, although there are sometimes disagreements on exactly what a given tail movement means. In general, a tail carried high is regarded as a sign of well-being or contentment. A tail that is swishing from side to side is seen as a warning signal. If a cat holds its tail close to its body and somewhat wrapped around it, a strong element of insecurity is probably being indicated. There are clearly degrees of all these movements—subtleties that only another cat is likely to be able to grasp.

39

Sneer Delight

Q. My cat Randall sometimes gets a strange, sneering grimace on his face when I give him catnip or even certain special foods. He looks as though he doesn't like the smell, but he also gets very excited. *What do these sneering expressions mean?*

A. They mean your cat is in absolute ecstasy. The grimace is called a "flehmen." In uncastrated males, the flehmen is particularly connected with sexual odors, but castrated males sometimes display it when confronted with especially delicious food odors. Any cat may display this expression in reaction to catnip. The grimace occurs in part because the cat is putting its tongue to the roof of its mouth in order to convey the odor to what is called Jacobson's organ. This organ is supplemental to the regular taste and scent organs. Many mammals have it, but it does not exist in humans.

40

A Fine How-de-do

Q. My cat sometimes gets up in my lap and puts his nose up to mine, which is very sweet. But then Barnaby often turns around and lifts his tail, exposing his anus. If I push him down, he gets quite cross. *How can I cure my cat of the bad habit of presenting his rear end to me and sometimes even guests?*

A. You can't, because this isn't a bad habit but utterly natural behavior. Cats often greet one another in this manner, sniffing noses first, with the more submissive cat then presenting the anus to be sniffed. As Muriel Beadle, author of *The Cat*, puts it, pushing down a cat's rump in this situation "is as rude as to refuse to shake a proffered human hand." You don't have to go as far as sniffing, of course, but you must let your cat present himself.

41

Twitch That Ear

Q. I am one of those odd people who can wiggle his ears, but I certainly can't keep up with my cat. *What makes the ears of a cat so flexible—is it less cartilage or more muscles?*

A. Both. The cartilage in a cat's ear is thinner, more flexible, and stands upright instead of lying close to the head. But there's also a tremendous difference in muscle complexity. Usually, the human ear has six muscles (you may have more since you can wiggle yours), while a cat's ear has four to five times as many muscles, between twenty and thirty depending on the breed.

42

The Din of Music

Q. My son has suddenly at the age of twelve discovered the supposed joys of rock music. When my husband and I are home we insist that he keep the volume at a level that permits adult thinking to proceed, but I'm sure he plays it at earsplitting levels when we are out. And I'm a bit worried about what that is doing to our cat, who seems to be extremely nervous lately and has also taken to hiding from us. *Can very loud music adversely affect a cat?*

A. It certainly can. Cats have forty thousand fibers in the aural nerve as opposed to the thirty thousand human beings have. They hear better and at higher frequencies than we do. That also means that they experience aural pain at lower levels than we do. Very loud music can not only cause behavioral changes in cats, but has also been known to give them ulcers. Tell your son he is making your cat's life a nightmare, never mind what he's doing to his own ears.

43

Belling the Cat

Q. I bought a collar with a small bell on it in order to keep better track of my cat when she is wandering outdoors. A neighbor called me up and said this was cruel. *Does a bell on a collar really bother a cat?*

A. Yes. You couldn't drive a cat any crazier if you tied a tin can to its tail. The incessant tinkling not only irritates a cat but also interferes with its finely attuned sense of hearing to a degree that is disorienting. Throw the bell away.

44

The Noise Not Heard

Q. I live in a prewar apartment building with very thick walls. I can seldom hear noise from an adjoining apartment unless the windows are open in both my apartment and the one next to or below mine. Last winter, however, an extraordinary thing happened. The windows were of course closed. But around midnight my cat became extremely agitated and started making strange sounds and running around in all directions. These weren't the usual evening "crazies." My cat seemed quite frightened. The next day I discovered that the young woman in the apartment next to mine had been strangled to death around midnight, apparently by an ex-boyfriend. *Is it possible for a cat to hear noises that a human being cannot, or is some "sixth sense" involved in a cat's reaction to strange or violent events in another apartment?*

A. Stories of this kind—and they are more common than you might think—always create a creepy feeling in human beings and add to the mysteriousness of cats. It has been scientifically proven that cats have extraordinary hearing, although the exact degree of sensitivity and how much it exceeds human hearing is an open question. It is not impossible that they may indeed have a "sixth sense" as well. American research, with its pragmatic emphasis, has largely ignored the area of "psychic" phenomena since Dr. J. B. Rhine's experiments a half century ago. Both Rhine and Russian scientists, who have taken psychic research much more seriously, found strong circumstantial evidence that cats may indeed have some abilities in this area, but hard proof is elusive.

45

Weather Cats?

Q. I've recently realized that when my cat wets a paw and rubs it against the back of his ear in a certain way, it always rains shortly thereafter, even though the sky may be clear when my cat makes this gesture. *Can cats predict rain?*

A. This is one of those questions that people get argumentative about. A great many people, including quite a few cat experts, do believe that cats can predict rain. But there are other experts, usually with a particularly science-oriented background, who get huffy about the whole idea and say cat lovers are overinterpreting. It's difficult to know what these experts are so upset about. After all, there's little question that cows lie down, to make sure they have a patch of dry grass beneath them, before rain clouds appear. Birds start returning to their nesting grounds considerably before rain begins. And then there are those "war wounds" and arthritic joints that many people claim start to hurt before the advent of rain. Perhaps what bothers the scientific types is the word "predict." They might even go along if it were put something like this: "Cats sometimes exhibit characteristic behavior patterns in response to coming changes in the weather, possibly because they are more in tune to changes in barometric pressure than we are."

The belief that cats can predict rain goes back as far as the ancient Egyptians. Some things are "known" that cannot be proved.

46

Earthquake Coming?

.*:

Q. I live in San Francisco, and my cat went absolutely nuts about ten minutes before the big World Series quake hit in 1989. *Do cats know an earthquake is coming before we do?*

A. This used to be regarded as a myth, but it is now fully accepted by seismologists that cats can indeed sense the vibrations of an earthquake before it actually hits. It is not known whether a cat's reaction becomes more disturbed according to the magnitude of the earthquake, but tests are being conducted to find out.

47

Dream On

***

Q. Sometimes when my cat is asleep she twitches, and her eyes seem to be moving under the closed lids. *Does my cat really have dreams?*

A. Most certainly. The movement of the eyes signifies what is called REM (rapid eye movement) sleep, which is the stage of sleep in which human beings as well as dogs and cats dream. This isn't just a guess based on external observation. The electrical activity in a cat's brain during REM sleep is consistent with what happens to human beings in the same stage of sleep. What do cats dream of? Ah, there's the rub. Even human beings who make a strong effort to recall their dreams, recording them right away if they wake during the night, are unable to remember more than a small portion of their dream activity. Dreams belong to the dreamer, and that includes a dreaming cat.

48

That Vacant Stare

Q. I'm a first-time cat owner. I grew up with dogs but I've always liked cats too. Since I now live in New York City, a cat seemed a more sensible pet and I've been finding my mixed-breed marmalade much more companionable than I, as a former "dog person," really expected. One thing that perplexes me, though, is how much time my friend Dundee spends staring into space in a kind of vacant-eyed way. *Why do a cat's eyes seem so much less focused than a dog's?*

A. In the reverse of what you might think, it's because cats see so much better. Dogs have a binocular field of vision of only 83 degrees; for a cat it's 120 degrees. This gives a cat terrific peripheral vision, allowing it to encompass a virtually cinemascopic field without focusing. When a cat does focus in a way that is more "doglike," it usually means that it is about to pounce, or at least thinking about it.

49

Color Me Uninterested

🐾

Q. When I read, I often put a pillow in my lap to support the book. There are two different pillows I use for this purpose, one red and one green. My cat seems much more interested in leaping up into my lap when I use the red pillow. *Are cats really color-blind, as so many people say?*

A. Animal behaviorists and biologists spent a good fifty years arguing about this subject from the start of World War I to the 1970s. The behaviorists thought they had proved that cats were color-blind, but with improved techniques the biologists were able to show that cats ought to be able to see color on the basis of the composition of their eyes. So the behaviorists tried new approaches over longer periods of time. The ultimate conclusion was that cats do have the capacity to distinguish between some colors, but that they have no good reason to do so and simply don't care. It can take thousands of tests using food as a "bait" to train a cat to put its latent ability to distinguish color to use. Your cat may prefer the red pillow, but it is almost certainly for reasons other than its color.

50

Eyes in the Night

Q. I have a degree of night blindness and since I live in a rather large house, I have a number of small night-lights scattered through the rooms. The eyes of my two cats seem to pick up this small amount of light and practically blaze away when they are in the right position vis-à-vis the light. But one of the cats always appears to have a red shine to its eyes and the other a kind of yellow-green shine. Maybe this is my own peculiar eyes playing tricks on me, but I don't think so. A friend tells me cats' eyes actually contain traces of some metal. *What is it that makes a cat's eyes shine so brightly in the dark?*

A. Your friend is right. There are several layers of cells in your cats' retinas that contain zinc and protein intermixed. This material is called *tapetum lucidem*. The material does not glow of its own accord, like phosphorous, but is instead a reflective material. There must be some light for the shine to appear. The reason the colors are different is that a color shift occurs, analogous to the difference between the negative and the print of a color photograph. Thus cats with blue or green eyes will have a red shine; cats with gold or copper eyes tend to have a greenish tinge.

51

Through the Darkness

🐾

Q. I'm told that cats can't really see in total darkness, but there's no question that my Max the Manx can see in what seems like total darkness to me. During a recent blackout after a bad storm, he even helped me find my way to another room where a flashlight was! *How much better than human beings can cats see in the dark?*

A. A number of experiments have been carried out to determine the answer to this question. The results have shown that a cat's eyes are at least six times more sensitive than human eyes to even diffused light in the dark. It may be that the light sensitivity of the cat is even greater, but allowances must be made for their more acute hearing and the "radar" that's provided by their whiskers.

52

A Touch of Affection

Q. My cat Tyger loves to be petted—up to a point. Sometimes he turns over on his back in my lap with his paws in the air. If I play with the fur under his chin, he's very happy, but if I try to rub his stomach, he gets very annoyed and sometimes even tries to scratch me. *Why is it that a lot of cats don't like to have their stomachs rubbed?*

A. For a cat, affection, both given and received, is very closely tied up with the sense of touch. Most experts believe that the care given to kittens by the mother cat is crucial to the development of this correlation between touch and affection. Thus a cat that does not like to be touched too much is likely to have had a disinterested or neglectful mother. But even cats that have had a good mother may become wary of touch if they have been kept out of the house or if they have been on their own as strays for any length of time.

In the case of your cat's not liking to have its stomach rubbed, however, the explanation is of a different kind. Lying on the back with the stomach exposed is a submissive posture, used by a cat to indicate to another cat that the dominance of the other cat has been accepted. Male cats in particular may adopt this posture with an owner, but then take offense if the stomach is actually touched. The submissive posture is expected in and of itself to be sufficiently craven. To touch the stomach is to go too far in asserting dominance.

53

Lick, Lick, Lick

Q. I realize that the chief reason cats lick themselves is to keep clean. But my cat also licks herself right after she has been sitting in someone's lap. At other times, the licking seems to be a nervous reaction, for instance after being scolded. *How much of the self-grooming cats do is for physical reasons and how much of it is psychological?*

A. I don't think anyone would want to venture percentages in answer to this question, but certainly both physical and psychological factors are involved. When a cat licks itself after being fondled, it may be doing two things at once: smoothing its fur and removing the scent of the person who was petting it, with the latter perhaps as much a matter of pleasure as cleanliness. It has recently been suggested that cats are not only cleaning themselves when they groom but also acquiring vitamin D, which is believed to be synthesized by the cat's skin in reaction to sunlight.

As to the grooming that takes place after a cat has been scolded or is otherwise upset, this is clearly related to the calming effect the mother's grooming has on newborn kittens. It's a security lick.

54

So Delicate and So Rough

Q. I've had both cats and dogs, and it has always intrigued me that the tiny cat's tongue is rougher than that of the dog. *Is there a special reason for the roughness of a cat's tongue?*

A. Yes. Pink and delicate as it looks, the cat's tongue has hundreds of small "hooks" on it. When a cat is eating prey it has caught, those hooks apparently become more erect and can actually be used to help tear at the flesh of the prey.

55

Falling on Your Feet

Q. My cat fell from a second-story window and broke a leg. Yet a woman I know in the neighborhood claims her cat fell six stories and was shaken up but not otherwise hurt. This doesn't make sense to me. *How far can a cat fall and survive, and is it possible for one cat to fall a lot farther than another and not be hurt as much?*

A. There has been a great deal of controversy on this issue. Twenty-five years ago, Fernand Méry, a French expert on cats whose books were translated into English and other languages, stated that cats that fell lesser distances from buildings were more likely to be hurt than those that fell from higher floors, up to and including the sixth floor. In subsequent years, a number of cat experts took strong issue with this statement, one of the most respected experts going so far as to deride him by name.

But, just to show that there is no such thing as the last word in the world of cats, it now looks as though Méry was correct, at least in general. The staff of the Animal Medical Center in New York City, which is a twenty-four-hour facility and thus is especially likely to deal with cats that have fallen out of windows, went through years of records and found that cats falling from higher floors often were not as badly injured.

Any cat that falls from a window will go through the same series of physical reactions in attempting to right itself. The cat first twists its head around into proper alignment, making use of both vision and inner ear balance. The spine follows, and then the rear. All this occurs within seconds. It is because it happens so fast that many experts refused to accept Méry's statement. If a cat can right itself when dropped from three

74

feet, then it should certainly not have more of a problem falling and landing from ten feet than from forty feet. Right? Well, no. Because something else happens when a cat falls from a greater height. It relaxes and goes into free fall, spreading its body somewhat to ride the air. The cat that falls from a lesser height does not have time to do this and is also likely to be much more tensed when it hits the ground. Thus the cat that has fallen from the lesser height may well hit the ground in a much more rigid posture that increases the chances of injury.

The maximum height from which a cat can fall and survive is now judged to be 120 feet. But that is unusual, and survival will depend on many other factors, from air currents to the surface on which the cat lands. In addition, if the cat is in a vertical instead of a horizontal position (upside down is still horizontal) when the fall begins, it will have a much harder time positioning itself for a proper landing, which requires that the back be arched.

56

Backward Down the Tree

🐾

Q. I have a cat that is forever getting itself marooned up in one tree or another. It sits there and yowls pitifully. I used to get frantic about it, and bought an extension ladder that made it possible for me to usually reach the cat, although at considerable risk to life and limb. Then one time, as I got within reaching distance, Martha climbed up even higher. I was furious and decided to leave her there for a while. A couple of hours later she reappeared on the porch. Since then I have never gotten out the extension ladder, but the odd thing is that I have never seen her actually in the process of coming down. *How do cats get down out of trees and why are they so reluctant to do it?*

A. They get down out of trees backward, which answers both your questions. It is an extremely undignified procedure, and without attributing a human emotion to cats, there is little question that they dislike having little control over a situation. Animals like squirrels that scamper down trees headfirst have a different claw configuration, not to mention a much heavier tail with which to balance themselves.

57
Hot Tin Roofs and All That

Q. We live in Florida and have a small terrace tiled with beautiful ceramic tiles from Spain. Alas, in summer the tiles get so hot when the sun is on them that we can't stand to walk barefoot. Our cat Trixie, however, loves to lie on this blistering surface. It makes me think that Tennessee Williams goofed when he named his play *Cat on a Hot Tin Roof.* Can cats stand much hotter temperatures than humans?

A. "Nervous as a cat on a hot tin roof" is an old Southern folk expression, but in fact cats can stand hotter temperatures than we can. Humans feel pain at 112 degrees; cats don't get jumpy until 124 degrees. Some cats are so oblivious to heat they don't even notice when their fur is being singed. But two parts of the cat's body, the nose and the lips, are temperature sensitive. A cat won't therefore eat food that is too hot, any more than we would.

58

Burying the Evidence

Q. I have four cats, two males and two females. Both of the females are Angoras. One male is a rather small colorpoint shorthair, the other a large Maine coon. All are neutered. The Angoras use the same litter box, but there are two separate ones for the males. Occasionally I go away for a weekend, leaving plenty of dry food and water, and the cats seem to do fine, with one exception. When I am away the Maine coon does not bury its feces but leaves them in little piles on top of the cat litter. It almost looks as though he has built up the litter around the feces. As a result, the house always smells a little. Am I being punished? *Don't cats have an innate drive to bury their feces?*

A. To say that your Maine coon is punishing you is a little anthropomorphic, but it may be that he is registering his displeasure. Cats can sometimes become entirely unhousebroken if they are sufficiently upset. But there may be another explanation here. It has long been a truism that cats have an innate drive to bury their feces, but Desmond Morris cites studies of wild cats showing that the dominant male in a given area actually displays his feces at strategic points, as though to emphasize his authority. Thus it could be that when you are away, the Maine coon decides to demonstrate that in your absence he is in charge. In other words, this unusual behavior may be directed not at you but at the other cats in the household.

59

Peeing in Private

Q. Late last spring we got a new kitten. We put her litter box in the family game room, and she took to it right away. It's now November and she has suddenly started avoiding the litter box and making messes around the house. I wondered if it could have anything to do with the fact that with cold weather the game room is used much more by my children and their friends. *Do cats need privacy in order to use a litter box?*

A. I'm sure you've hit on the nature of the problem. Some cats don't seem to mind where the litter box is. But many cats are remarkably private in nature and will refuse to use a litter box in a noisy or busy area of the house. This is especially true if the area was quiet when the cat was first trained to the litter box and a major change takes place in that environment.

You will have to move the litter box to a quieter spot and retrain your cat. While you are getting her used to the new location, it is a good idea to change the litter at least twice a day.

60

In Harness

Q. I've always heard that cats take badly to being walked on a leash, but occasionally I do see one out for a stroll with its owner. *Can a cat be trained to walk on a leash?*

A. If you start training a cat when it is still a kitten—the sooner the better—it is sometimes possible to train a cat to a leash. But you are really attempting to make the cat do something unnatural, and even early training doesn't work in many cases. With an adult cat it is pretty much hopeless. Cats dislike leashes so much that they often just sit down and refuse to budge. Beyond that, the idea of sticking to a straight line, unless a cat is on a fence top or tree limb, is completely alien to the nature of the animal. A dog off a leash will often trot along in a straight line of its own accord for some distance. A cat will meander all over the place.

If you do attempt to train a kitten to a leash, use a harness.

Not only does it give better results, but it prevents the cat from slipping its collar. On the other hand, if you have a cat that is allowed outdoors on its own on a regular basis in a town or suburban setting, it should have a collar with an identifying tag, but the collar should be made of a stretch fabric so that it *can* be slipped off should the cat get caught on a wire fence or branch. A cat with a tight leather collar can end up hanging itself.

61

Hide-and-Seek

Q. I have two cats, one of which loves to climb into small spaces, from a dresser drawer to a clothes hamper, when you have your back turned. The other almost never does this, and in fact seems to love to lie around in open spaces where he can be tripped over. Both cats are males. *Is there any explanation of this difference in behavior?*

A. If there is, it is lost in the evolutionary mists. There do, however, seem to be a greater number of cats that like to play hide-and-seek, as it were, and if this is true of your cat, a little extra care must be taken. Whenever closing anything that has been open, always check to make sure that your cat hasn't taken up surreptitious residence. This is particularly true of major appliances like refrigerators, washers, and driers. Tragedy can result if a cat is trapped in any of these machines.

62

Catnip Trip

Q. I have two cats, one male and one female. The male goes absolutely bananas when given catnip, but the female doesn't seem interested. *What is it about catnip that excites cats and why doesn't it have the same effect on them all?*

A. Catnip is a member of the mint family, but it contains an oil that causes some cats to get "high." In 1972, R. C. Hatch, a Canadian researcher, reported in *The American Journal of Veterinary Research* that the chemical structure of the active ingredient in catnip is very similar to that of LSD. Whether or not a cat is susceptible to catnip is a matter of genetics. It involves a recessive gene so that two kittens in the same litter may have different responses to the drug. Most veterinarians advise using catnip sparingly. This is one area in which it is safe to talk about cat behavior in human terms: Even a cat can have a "bad trip." There is some evidence to suggest that among the susceptible cats, males are more affected than females.

63

My Cat's Gone Mad

Q. I am new to cat owning. I have a year-old female American shorthair that's an absolute delight. But every so often she seems to go absolutely nuts and tears around the house like a whirling dervish. *Is there some specific thing that sets my cat off when she races around like a mad creature, and is it anything to worry about?*

A. No one is quite sure why cats occasionally get the "crazies," as they are usually called, but it is something almost all cats do and nothing to worry about. It's similar to a dog suddenly chasing its own tail, but often considerably more dramatic. Just relax and enjoy the show.

64

Faster Than a Speeding Dog

Q. I live in a residential area of widely spaced houses where pets, both dogs and cats, are allowed outdoors on their own on a regular basis. I have a wirehaired terrier that has taken to chasing the cat of a new neighbor a couple of houses down. The neighbor's wife has fits about it and says I ought to fence my dog in. My answer is that she doesn't have to worry, my terrier will never catch her cat. *Isn't it true that a cat can run faster than many dogs?*

A. I agree that your neighbor's cat is probably safe. A cat can certainly outrun a dog its own size or slightly larger, and even some very large, lumbering kinds of dogs, at least over short distances. And usually a cat needs to go only a short distance before it comes upon a tree, fence, shed roof, or other aboveground perch where it can shelter itself. It should also be noted that some cats appear to be the instigator of this kind of chase. I once had two cats that provoked utterly different reactions from a neighbor's dog. One was constantly being chased, the other never. It was very clear that the cat that got chased was taunting the dog, playing a "catch me if you can, yah, yah" kind of game.

65

Wandering Tom

Q. I have a cat that adopted me. At least I think I have a cat. It's a marmalade male, neutered, that showed up on the terrace one day a couple of years ago. He stayed for two months, but then disappeared for ten days. Sometimes he's here, sometimes not. He always seems well fed when he shows up again. *Is a cat that seems to regard you as its owner but keeps disappearing a stray cat or does it have more than one home?*

A. If your wandering Tom is always well fed and in good shape, he probably has more than one home. He may even have three or more. These cats are charmers and very smart, moving around to visit their various great friends without ever quite adhering to one household. There are people who do this, too, you know. But they are seldom anybody's cat but their own.

66

The Welcome Home Cat

❧

Q. My wife and I have both noticed that our Siamese cat Silky can predict when one or the other of us is coming home, even if it is an unusual time. He rushes to the front door of our apartment and is waiting there when we open the door. We've each seen him do this for the other. We live in a high-rise building, but it can't be the noise of the elevator that tips him off, since there are six other apartments on the same floor, and the elevator is always opening and closing without his paying the slightest attention. I hate to say it, but it's almost as though he's psychic. *How do cats figure out that an owner is about to come home without any real clues?*

A. The number of cat owners that suspect their cats of being psychic is large indeed. It is even possible that they are—this is an area of research that has been largely neglected by pragmatic Americans, but Russian scientists have long been interested in the possibility of psychic connections between pets and their owners. The most usual explanation put forward by American experts is that it has to do with sounds that humans can't hear or at least can't quantify easily. It should be noted that many cats give little evidence of having such abilities, at least in regard to the return of the owner.

If you want a cat that has phenomenal abilities in this regard, get yourself a Japanese bobtail. Not only are cats of this breed likely to be waiting for you, they also have an endearing trait of greeting the owner with one paw raised.

67

Southpaws

Q. My wife named our cat Sandy, after the actress Sandy Duncan, but I think that even though the cat is a female, she really takes after the great left-handed pitcher Sandy Koufax. I swear she's a left-handed cat. She always seems to lead with her left paw, and if you throw a ball at her, she swipes at it with her left paw. *How common are left-handed cats?*

A. Left-handedness is much more common in cats than in human beings. One study by a British physiologist, J. Cole, showed that 58 percent of cats have a strong bias toward the use of one paw, with twice as many favoring the left paw as the right one. There is some evidence, by the way, that the slang baseball term "southpaw" for left-handers was derived from observation of cats. In baseball parlance, southpaws are often looked upon as "strange cats."

68

Performing Cats?

Q. My cat sometimes extends a paw as though to shake hands. *Can I train my cat to shake hands when I ask her to or to perform other tricks?*

A. Yes, you can, if you are a professional animal trainer and are willing to spend several hours a day working with your cat. Otherwise, forget it. Many cats have a proclivity to repeat certain playful gestures, when they feel like it, that can pass for "tricks." Be content with that.

69

Mirror Mysteries

Q. I'm thirteen and I have a cat named Mantha. Her real name is Samantha, but my older brother kept calling her Sam, so now it's Mantha. My older brother has a dog, and he says dogs are smarter than cats because a dog can recognize itself in a mirror and a cat can't. *Why doesn't my cat know it's her face in the mirror?*

A. Even experts aren't certain why cats and dogs react to mirrors so differently, but it's not a matter of relative smartness. A cat will see its reflection in a mirror and try to touch it with a paw, or even hiss at it. It seems to be fooled into thinking it is another cat. A dog will virtually ignore its own reflection, but whether that means it actually recognizes itself is not certain.

These different reactions seem to be connected with how cats and dogs respond to objects in motion and at rest in general. A hunting dog can be trained to stop dead in its tracks and "point" at an animal that isn't moving at all. A cat, on the other hand, shows little interest in prey unless it is moving. Thus, what excites the cat about its reflection is the motion it sees—each time the cat moves so does the reflection. It's not a matter of smart or dumb but of being attuned to the world in a different way.

70

Trapped!

Q. Our cat managed to get himself trapped in a crawl space in our apartment building—we're still not sure how. It was three days before we found him. There was a pipe with a very slow leak in the space, so he must have had some water, but certainly no food. *How long can a cat survive without food?*

A. That would depend on the health of the cat and the availability of at least minimum moisture. But cats in the wild can survive a number of days without food when there is an absence of prey; it's bred into them. Domestic cats also play it very smart when they are trapped. They become extremely quiet in order to conserve energy, but that may have a downside in that it makes them harder to locate.

71

No, You're a Kitten

*:

Q. When I wake up in the morning, my cat has always deposited two or three items at the side of my bed—a sock, a pencil, one small item or another. She's strictly an indoor cat, so I assume this isn't the same thing as an outdoor cat bringing a mouse to you. *When a cat brings you inanimate objects is it trying to please you as a master or parent?*

A. A number of experts in animal behavior believe that almost the exact opposite is going on. The cat is the parent, in this situation, and you're the kitten. The behavior is in fact like that of an outdoor cat bringing its owner a mouse, but the cat has been forced to find substitutes. A feral cat—or even a farm cat—will devour its prey unless it has kittens, in which case, after weaning, it will bring food to the litter. But a cat that is primarily a pet will often display this kind of mothering behavior toward its owner.

You can turn this kind of behavior in a cat into an ongoing game. If you have a cellar, garage, or other enclosed area that your cat has the run of, you can hide objects like athletic socks or old gloves for the cat to find and bring to you, then hide them again for it to find again. There are owners who report playing this kind of game for the entire life of a cat. But not all cats will play the game. If you have more than one cat, it is perfectly possible that one will participate while the other shows total disinterest.

72

Time for a Bath?

🐾

Q. My Russian blue Lara absolutely hates to have a bath. She looks spectacular afterward, but I sometimes wonder if it is worth the trauma, not only for her but for me. *How often should a cat be bathed?*

A. This is another of those whom-do-you-believe areas of cat care. Some experts say that a cat should never be bathed unless it manages to cover itself with something so gooey or possibly dangerous to its health that it can't be expected to clean itself properly. Others feel that a cat should be bathed regularly, although that may mean once a month or once every six weeks.

Some cats do not mind being bathed; others loathe it. This difference does not necessarily seem to depend on how young the cat is when it is first bathed, but there are some indications that an early start does help to accustom the cat to the process. It should also be noted that some outdoor cats like to dirty themselves up by rolling in dirt when they think nobody is looking, and a cat like that may need to be bathed more often than another. Ultimately, bathing a cat comes down to practicality and common sense. If a cat hates being bathed and the chief reason for doing it is the owner's aesthetic pleasure, I think it's wise to reconsider, as you are doing.

73

Best Friends Fighting

Q. I have two cats, both males, which were acquired about a year apart. After an initial phase that was difficult, Bob and Bing became great friends, virtually inseparable. A few days ago, a door blew open and Bob slipped out (both are indoor cats). It only took me ten minutes to find Bob, in a little stand of trees at the back of the house, but when I brought him back in Bing attacked him as though he were a complete stranger. *What causes cats that have always gotten along to suddenly get into a fight?*

A. In your case, you have supplied your own answer. In that stand of trees, Bob obviously picked up the scent of another cat. When you brought him back in Bing attacked the smell of that stranger. This can also happen if you take one cat to the vet and not the other, or if someone else who has a cat or a dog handles one pet and not the other. This is one situation where a bath is in order for the cat that has picked up the alien smell.

74

Bird Catching

Q. My cat Sergio is a bird chaser. He tries and tries to catch them, but they are almost always too quick for him, and the look of frustration on his face is really quite comical. But then once in a while I have to chastise myself for being amused: Sergio actually catches a bird and brings it back to me. *How many birds actually are killed by cats?*

A. The bird-chasing aspect of a cat's nature gives a lot of people pause. Fortunately, cats really aren't very good at catching birds. A number of studies have been done on this subject, some more scientific than others, and the results vary, with 15 to 25 percent of cats' prey consisting of birds in various parts of the world. The variations may have more to do with the kinds of birds found in different locations than anything else. Some birds spend more time on the ground than others and are less quick at making a takeoff—or a getaway. Cats in general are not terribly good at catching birds. They like to pounce, and do not expect the prey to leave the ground. Some experts claim that cats that do become adept at bird catching are likely to change their habits and concentrate on birds, ignoring rodents. Given the expressions of frustration that all cat observers have noted on the faces of unsuccessful bird hunters, it may be that those that are good at it derive a special satisfaction from such hunting.

Butterfly Hunting

Q. I live in a part of northern Florida where we have a profusion of butterflies. I believe we're in the middle of a migratory route for several of them. My cat is constantly chasing them, which rather distresses me, although he seems to be having a wonderful time. I don't think he catches many, however. *Why would a cat chase something that it can't catch and which would hardly supply enough nutrients to make up for the energy expended in catching them?*

A. Cats love to chase butterflies. It's not the color that tempts them, of course; we've seen that cats don't care about color. It's the motion of the butterfly that seems so tempting, often low to the ground and seemingly quite slow. But you're right, cats are terrible at actually catching butterflies. The cat tends to leap for the butterfly, and with its foot off the ground, the cat's ability to control its direction is no match for the rapid darting of the butterfly. Cats generally give up on things they can't succeed at, but the endless pursuit of the elusive butterfly is obviously an exception. It may simply be a form of play.

76

Wide-eyed with Hunger

Q. I know this sounds like something out of *Garfield*, but I swear that when my cat approaches her feeding bowl her eyes seem to get much bigger. *Do cats' eyes change when they are about to eat?*

A. Yes, the pupils of a cat's eyes may enlarge by as much as four times their usual diameter when they approach their feeding bowl. Actually, human beings respond to pleasurable stimuli in the same way, but because the dilation is much less pronounced, we don't particularly notice it.

77

Moist, Semimoist, Dry

Q. The advertisements for cat food, especially on television, are often so cute that you want to rush out and buy the product just because you enjoyed the commercial. But there seem to be a lot of arguments among cat owners about what's really best for cats, canned food, the semimoist packets, or dry food. (I notice that often the same company makes all three.) *In terms of health and nutrition, is there any real difference between the three kinds of cat food?*

A. There are arguments among cat experts, too. But even veterinarians with different ideas on the subject take note that cat owners quite often appear to believe one set of claims over another largely in terms of their own convenience. Some people find opening a can of cat food the easiest thing to do. Moist (canned) foods contain a lot of water, which cuts down the need to change the cat's water bowl as often. Other cat owners like semimoist food because it is less smelly. People who often go away for weekends may prefer dry food because a large amount of it can be left out to be consumed over several days without spoiling, along with several bowls of water to provide enough moisture.

Provided the cat food you buy is clearly labeled as complete or scientifically balanced you are fairly safe with any choice—government regulations forbid using the word "complete" unless it's the truth, but beware of products that do not offer complete or balanced diets. Probably the most quoted expert on this subject is Dr. Michael W. Fox, who alternates dry food with canned food, and also gives his cat table scraps occasionally. There are veterinarians, however, who are strongly against table scraps. Dr. Fox, with his emphasis on variety, nevertheless makes sense to me.

78

A Mouseful at a Time

Q. The two cats I had in the past were fed canned food. My latest cat, however, presents a problem. He never eats more than a small amount at a time, and as the day wears on the food sometimes begins to smell rather strongly. I worry that it may be spoiling, and am thinking of switching to dry food. *Why do some cats eat only a small amount of food at a time?*

A. Many cats eat only a small amount at a time. What they are doing is taking in at each foray to the food dish an amount of food equivalent to the nutrition they would get from a single mouse. A barnyard cat may catch and devour as many as ten mice a day. Thus your cat is simply adhering to the normal eating pattern of a good mouser.

It should be noted that there are those who insist that a cat should have just one large meal a day; this, they claim, is natural because it is what lions do. Well, although there are lion characteristics that exist in domestic cats, the prey of each is entirely different. One of the staples of the lion's diet is the zebra, which can weigh two hundred pounds more than a lion, whereas it takes many a mouse to equal the weight of a domestic cat.

79

A Saucer of Cream

Q. As an occasional treat I give my cat a few teaspoons of cream in a saucer. My cat loves it, but a couple of friends of mine say cream and even milk really aren't good for cats. *Haven't people been giving cats cream for hundreds of years because it is good for them?*

A. People have been giving cats cream and milk for as long as cats have been pets, under the assumption that they were doing right by their cats. It has also been assumed that cats adore cream, to wit, Shakespeare's line from *Henry IV, Part I:* "I am as vigilant as a cat to steal cream." But assumptions are one thing, biological reality another. Milk and, especially, cream can cause diarrhea in cats. Some researchers believe that cats lack an enzyme that breaks down lactose in the stomach. Many cats, however, don't seem to have problems if the milk (not cream) is given in small amounts on an intermittent basis. Other cats, perhaps instinctively protecting themselves, actually shy away from milk after they are weaned. Many veterinarians advise not giving cats milk at all, others suggest diluting it with water. Certainly it should not be given very often, no matter what the folk history indicates, and if any sign of diarrhea appears, milk should not be offered at all.

80

Fish Stories

🐾

Q. I have always heard that cats like fish, but that doesn't make much sense to me. After all, most of the "big cats" live in rather arid areas where it's unlikely there will be any fish at all. *Where did the idea that cats like fish come from?*

A. Here again it's a matter of human beings' feeding cats a certain food, cats' becoming addicted to it, and a general statement being extrapolated from specific circumstances. There are in fact some species of wild cats that do feed on fish. But that doesn't mean all cats like fish. Some seem to become easily hooked on it, others don't like it at all. The latter are in fact the wiser cats since fish, especially the dark red tuna so often used in cat foods, contains a great deal of fat and can cause a disease called *steatis* that involves an inflammation of the fat tissues of cats. This can be counteracted by vitamin E, which is now added to all fish-based cat foods. Even so, a widely varied diet is much to be preferred.

81

Vegetarian Cats?

Q. As a vegetarian, it disturbs me to feed my cat meat. I understand that some new cat foods have been developed that are vegetarian but still provide a balanced diet. *Is there any reason not to feed a cat a special vegetarian diet?*

A. Yes! Please don't do this. Human beings are omnivores, which means we can eat just about anything that isn't toxic unless we have an allergy of some sort. Thus it is possible to develop a balanced diet for human beings that eschews meat altogether, substituting the protein from legumes. But cats are carnivores—flesh eaters. In the wild they do consume vegetable matter, but they get it in the form of undigested food in the stomachs of their prey. (I'm sorry if this makes you queasy, but facts are facts.) Many cats are fed too much meat, it is true, which can create other health problems, but to deprive a cat of meat (or the meat extracts in dry food) altogether is to endanger its health. Some cat experts go so far as to call it animal abuse.

82

That Cat Is No Dog

Q. I have a friend who has two dogs and a cat. She feeds all three of them dog food, plus some table scraps. The cat seems healthy, but this still seems wrong to me. *Don't cats have very different nutritional needs from dogs?*

A. Yes. A cat needs almost twice as much protein as a dog, although many people assume it's the other way around. A cat also has much less need for carbohydrates. It may be that your friend is getting away with feeding her cat dog food because the table scraps she offers are helping to balance things out. But she is asking for trouble down the line.

83

The Well-Fed
Ratcatcher

Q. My wife and I recently bought a run-down farm in rural Pennsylvania, which we are gradually fixing up. A neighbor sold us a fifteen-week-old cat that he said had already been trained as a ratcatcher by its mother, something we sorely need since the barn in particular has a thriving rodent population. He told us that we should keep the cat well fed with dry food. This sounds strange to us. *If a cat is well fed why would it bother to hunt rats and mice?*

A. Your neighbor knows whereof he speaks. First, cats hunt not only for food but also for sport. Rat catching takes a lot of energy, and a well-fed cat will be more inclined to hunt. In addition, by feeding the cat yourself you will help preserve the cat's domestic nature. Left entirely to itself, it could well become an essentially feral cat. Since your cat has been trained by an expert mother, it sounds as though you have yourself a good bargain.

84

A Pot of Grass (Not *That* Kind)

:

Q. We have a long-haired, although not purebred, indoor cat. It's been suggested to us that we should keep a pot of lawn grass growing by a window where the cat can get at it, as chewing on grass can help the cat deal better with hair balls, aiding in regurgitating them. *Is it true that cats need grass to get hair balls up or do they perhaps derive some nutritional value from the grass?*

A. Some experts insist that cats eat grass to help in the regurgitation of hair balls. Others believe this is secondary to some nutritional need—Desmond Morris pinpoints folic acid as the requirement, noting that it is important to the formation of hemoglobin. Still others suggest both these factors may play a part, and that grass may be important for reasons we really don't understand. At any rate, it can't hurt to bring a little lawn into your house.

85

Taking Off Excess Ounces

🐾

Q. My cat sometimes goes through a period during which she eats considerably less than usual. She seems quite normal otherwise, but I wonder if there could be something hidden that is wrong with her. *Is it normal for a cat to go through periods of eating less?*

A. Certainly. To begin with, food intake normally increases in cold weather and decreases in hot weather. An indoor cat living in an apartment or house that is automatically temperature controlled, where the temperature remains fairly constant regardless of the season, will be less likely to follow this pattern for obvious reasons. But it may still go through periods of eating less—because it is going on a self-imposed diet to remain at an optimal weight, though cats are less likely to do this as they get older. Cats that become clearly overweight, however, have usually been cajoled into becoming food junkies by their indulgent owners. Some overweight cats may have glandular disturbances, but there is no solid evidence to suggest that the neutering of either the female or the male necessarily leads to cat obesity.

In terms of food quantity, please remember that while some variation in appetite is normal, a cat that refuses to eat is almost certainly ill and should be taken to the vet right away.

86

Stones from Ash

♣

Q. I have been told that I am likely to give my tomcat stones that could block the urinary track by feeding it only dry cat food because there is so much ash in the food. *Is it true that the ash content of dry food can give my cat health problems?*

A. Most veterinarians say no. It is true that dry cat food has a fairly high ash content, but a great many experiments have failed to prove that this is a problem. Some cats are simply more prone to stones than others, regardless of what they eat. Male cats are likely to have more problems with urinary blockages because the length and narrowness of the urethra can make it difficult to pass any stones that develop. Stones can also result from an episode of cystitis, a common infection of the bladder caused by bacteria.

87

Bad for the Bones

Q. I've decided to get a cat and I'm getting free advice from all sides. Some of it is contradictory, particularly about what a cat should be fed. For instance, some people say that cats adore liver and nothing could be better for them. Others say that it is bad for cats and should be avoided. *Should or should not a cat be fed a lot of liver?*

A. Before dealing with liver specifically, let's focus on the first myth that comes up in your question. Whenever people say that their cats adore any particular food, whether it is liver, tuna, or bananas, remember that they're talking about *their* own cats, not cats in general. The truth is that cats get hooked on certain foods—adore them—because they are what the owners give them. Cats in the wild can't afford to be finicky or they'd starve to death. Owners make cats finicky by giving them certain foods too often. The more variety there is to a cat's diet, the healthier it will be, and you won't run into the problem of having it refuse to eat when the diet needs to be changed for medical reasons.

As to liver itself, it should *not* be given to your cat often, certainly no more than every ten days. Liver contains a lot of phosphorus and is rich in vitamin A. Both phosphorus and vitamin A will weaken a cat's bones when present in excess. Liver flavoring, however, causes no harm—just be sure to read the label carefully.

88

Thanksgiving Menaces

Q. On Thanksgiving I always lock our two cats in a back bedroom an hour before the feast is served until after the cleanup is finished. My sister-in-law thinks this is cruel. I think I'm looking out for the safety of my cats. It's always chaos in the kitchen on Thanksgiving, and I'm afraid the cats will get a hold of something that could hurt them. *Aren't turkey bones very dangerous for cats?*

A. A cat could easily choke on a turkey bone. Chicken bones are bad enough, but turkey bones are especially brittle, and even if a cat swallowed one without a problem, the sharp ends could cause internal bleeding. The string used to truss the turkey and the plastic pop-up thermometers that now come with many turkeys are also tempting to cats and carry their own dangers. You are a wise cat owner to lock your pets away on such a hectic day in the kitchen.

89

Poisonous Poinsettias

Q. Last summer we gave our seven-year-old daughter a kitten for her birthday. At Christmas I have always put a lot of red and white poinsettias around the house, but my mother-in-law says I mustn't do that anymore because poinsettias and a lot of other household plants can make the cat sick if she eats any of them. *Are there really ordinary houseplants that are poisonous to cats?*

A. I'm afraid your mother-in-law is right on this one. Poinsettias contain a sap that will inflame the mucous membranes of your cat's mouth, as well as the lining of the esophagus and the stomach. There are a number of other houseplants to be careful about, including another Christmas favorite, the amaryllis, which will bring on almost immediate vomiting. Caladiums can cause excessive production of saliva as well as swelling of the mouth; dieffenbachia will have the same effects, and may also temporarily paralyze the vocal chords.

In the yard there are a host of plants that can cause poisoning if eaten by a cat. Lily of the valley can bring on vomiting and an irregular heartbeat, larkspur convulsions as well as cardiovascular problems. Morning glories and periwinkles are hallucinogens and will make your cat act very strangely. But outdoor cats are much less likely to eat these plants than indoor cats are to take a nibble of a houseplant. Cats eat plants only out of curiosity, and there are so many plants outdoors that they are usually ignored—besides, there are better things to do, like chasing mice, birds, and butterflies. But the indoor cat is likely to be tempted. The answer is to hang plants near the ceiling or to screen them off behind glass or wire netting.

90

A Thread of Danger

Q. I am a knitter and my cat of course loves to chase balls of wool around. But the other day I left my knitting out while I had what turned out to be a very long telephone call, and when I returned to where I had left my knitting, my cat was choking on some of the yarn. *Is it normal for a cat to actually swallow yarn?*

A. Unfortunately, yes. Yarn, string, and sewing thread all may be swallowed by cats occasionally. Sometimes they ingest a fairly short piece that has been left lying around, and the owner doesn't realize what has happened. The consequences for a cat's stomach may be serious enough to require surgery. A piece of thread with a needle still attached to it can be a grave danger. It's important to think of your cat as a perpetual two-year-old child, capable of getting into anything, and take the necessary precautions.

91

Electrical Hazards

Q. I'm about to get a kitten. I remember that when I was a child, my aunt Helen used to disconnect any exposed electrical cords in the room where she left young cats whenever she went out. *How dangerous are electrical cords to cats and what can I do to protect my kitten?*

A. Some cats—not all—become fascinated by electrical cords when they are young, especially if the cords are in a tangle on the floor. To protect your kitten, make sure there are no loose tangles and tape the cords securely to the baseboard instead. If you see your cat chewing on an electrical cord, make a loud noise and throw a pillow or some other soft object at the cat. If there is any sign that a cat has bitten through a cord, *do not touch the cat*—you could get a bad shock yourself. Disconnect the cord before touching the cat, or move the cat away from it with a nonconducting object like a wooden cane.

If there are any burns around the cat's mouth, get it to a veterinarian immediately. Even if the burns seem minor, and the cat appears to recover quickly from the shock, still take the cat to a vet right away. Electric shock can cause a buildup of fluid in the lungs, called pulmonary edema, that can cause sudden death a few hours later. Don't take chances.

Cats often outgrow the cord-chewing inclination, especially if you warn them off at every opportunity. If you have a kitten that seems particularly prone to this dangerous form of play, you may indeed want to emulate your aunt Helen and disconnect the cords in a room when you leave the house.

92

Garage Poisons

Q. My cat is always sneaking into the garage. I know that there are a number of cleaning and automotive products that are poisonous to cats, and I try to keep things put away or firmly closed. *What products are especially dangerous and why would a cat want to taste them in the first place?*

A. Almost anything in a bottle, can, tube, or plastic container that you are likely to have in your garage is poisonous to cats. Everything of that nature, from a spare can of gasoline, kerosene for storm lamps, solvents, and rust removers to the boric acid used to clean car radiators, carries dangers. Cats are far more likely to ingest such chemicals than dogs are. In some cases, it is hard to tell why, but in some others, the attraction is obvious. For example, antifreeze, especially the common ethylene glycol formulation, attracts cats because the glycol has a sweet smell to it. Antifreeze is also particularly lethal—the death rate from it is over 85 percent.

All chemical compounds should be stored in cupboards that close securely. Don't forget drips and leaks on the garage floor. Clean them up immediately.

93

Poison First Aid

Q. Last week I found my cat panting and weaving around. I suspected she had swallowed something poisonous but couldn't immediately figure out what it was and rushed her to the vet. My vet took quick care of the problem (the culprit eventually turned out to be fabric softener), but when I asked him if there was anything I could have done at home, he said not to try because the remedy for one kind of poison could turn out to worsen the effects of another kind. *Is there really nothing you can do to help a cat that's been poisoned?*

A. You can induce a cat to vomit by giving it a teaspoon of 3 percent hydrogen peroxide solution (the dosage may have to be repeated). This is fine with a number of poisonous substances, including fabric softener, but it can make the situation much worse if the cat has swallowed a corrosive product like gasoline. Corrosives burn as they are going down, and bringing them back up will double the damage. So you really shouldn't do anything. It is much safer just to get the cat to the vet right away. If you have any evidence of what the poison is, take the container with you.

94

Temperature Testiness

Q. I'm confused. From talking to other cat owners, it seems that we're all being told different things by our veterinarians about what a normal temperature for a cat is. Some people say around 100 degrees, others say a degree higher, and not to worry if it goes down or up by a degree or two. *Is there a normal temperature for a cat?*

A. Don't blame your veterinarian. First, there is a great deal of debate about this issue. Second, it does seem to be generally true that a change of a degree doesn't have the same significance for cats that it does for humans. Third, *your* cat can be said to have a normal temperature; if you have two cats, however, they may have slightly different normal temperatures.

The issue is complicated by the fact that newborn kittens have temperatures down in the eighties. They huddle together and against the mother for warmth. A higher temperature would virtually burn them up since their metabolisms aren't yet in full operation. This fact alone indicates that temperature in a cat simply cannot be adopted as the same kind of guideline we use in judging human illness. A change of a degree shouldn't be a cause for worry; it may have no significance, medically speaking. If it's more than that, and accompanied by other signs of malaise, then you should begin to monitor the situation carefully.

95

Grooming Glooms

Q. Our family cat hasn't been grooming herself nearly as much lately. I took her to the vet and he said there was no physical problem. Our oldest son did go away to college a few weeks ago, and I've been missing him a lot. *Is it possible that because I'm feeling low the cat is too and isn't grooming herself because she's feeling sad?*

A. First, you were wise to take your cat to the vet for a checkup. A cat that stops grooming or cuts down on it a lot may well be ill—along with the refusal to eat, it is one of the most obvious signs of possible ill health. But I suspect you are right in your suggestion that the departure of your son is the problem here. Some experts pooh-pooh the idea that a cat can suffer depression, but it seems quite possible that your cat misses your son herself and is also picking up on your own low spirits. You can do both your cat and yourself a favor by giving her especially loving attention at this point.

96

A Real Danger Sign

Q. My tomcat had trouble urinating a couple of weeks ago. He seemed to be straining a good deal, but then after a day and a half he seemed fine again. But I worry about it. *When a cat strains to urinate is it a sign of something seriously wrong?*

A. It can be very serious. Your cat probably had a stone that he managed to pass. Stones are quite common among male cats, particularly castrated ones. The danger is that the cat may not succeed in passing the stone, and if the urethra is badly blocked, the cat can become very ill indeed. Sometimes a cat will even die from this problem due to urea poisoning. A cat that is straining to urinate should always be taken to a veterinarian at the earliest opportunity.

97

Cat Bites

Q. Our cat has suddenly taken up biting. He was declawed years ago, so it's not a substitute for using his claws. The only thing I can think of is that we've had the cellar, where he used to roam, shut off for a month because we're transforming it into a TV and music room. *Could a cat become upset enough about being kept out of a place it is used to going to turn to biting?*

A. It is possible. Cats are very territorial, and the cellar may have been a place that he regarded as particularly his. But it seems more likely that your cat has a hidden health problem. The sudden development of irritability in a usually docile cat is often a sign that there is something physically amiss. You should take your cat for a checkup.

In terms of your own health, you should pay careful attention to any bites you or other people receive. A cat bite often creates a puncture wound that is very small on the surface but goes fairly deep. The surface may heal over quickly while an infection develops underneath. If there is any sign of swelling, see your physician.

98

Scratching Posts

❧

Q. I am about to marry an enchanting woman who is a cat lover. She had an old cat that died recently, and she wants to get a kitten once we are married. I view this with some trepidation since I own a number of valuable antiques. My wife-to-be insists that she can train the kitten to use a scratching post, and that it is not necessary to have the cat declawed. *Can any cat be trained to use a scratching post and can it be done quickly enough to avoid damage to furniture?*

A. There are those who claim that any cat can be trained, but the reason so many cats are declawed is that scratching can be a very considerable problem. Advice on how to train a cat to use a scratching post abounds, but practically everyone seems to have slightly different ideas on the subject. Some suggest that the post be covered with carpet, others swear by cork, and still others vote for tree bark. Quite a number of experts warn that the material used to cover the post should be different from whatever it is that you don't want scratched—in other words, avoid the use of carpeting if your house has wall-to-wall carpeting already. It is generally agreed that the post must be well anchored and high enough so that the cat can stand up to scratch, which is the posture cats prefer. Training, which involves placing the cat in front of the post and moving its paws against it, should begin as soon as possible. How long it will take depends on the persistence of the owner and the nature of the cat. Some cats pick it up very quickly, others are extremely resistant.

Some experts say that what you should look for in buying a kitten is one whose mother is trained to a scratching post. If the kitten is left with the mother long enough, it is claimed, she will train the kitten herself.

99
Scratching Off the Old

Q. I bought a scratching post for my cat, and while he does use it, he still goes after the chair I most often use in the living room. Maybe if I better understood why he likes to scratch my chair, I could find a way to prevent it. *What is a cat trying to accomplish when it scratches furniture? Is it my odor that attracts it to the particular chair?*

A. Your cat is scratching in order to remove the old outer sheath from its front claws. This is not a matter of sharpening in the sense of honing a knife, as most people assume, but rather of removing the outer covering to reveal the new sharp claw underneath. The action has been compared to a snake's shedding its skin or the sharpening of a pencil.

As to why a cat is particularly attracted to its owner's customary chair, odor is certainly a part of it. In fact, some cat owners find that attaching a used sock to a scratching post helps to condition the cat to use it more often. But you should also understand that your cat is not just lured by your smell, it is also depositing *its* smell on the chair. The pads on the bottom of its feet contain scent glands; they produce an odor virtually undetectable to a human but very telling to a cat. In a sense, then, the cat is marking the chair as part of its territory—which, perhaps more than anything else, is why it is difficult to dissuade a cat from this practice.

100

The Declawing Wars

Q. I was having a nice catch-up conversation with an old friend who had lived abroad for several years. I happened to mention that I was having my cat declawed, and my friend almost shouted, "That's animal abuse." I practically dropped the phone, and the conversation went downhill from there. *Is there really so much controversy about declawing cats?*

A. Unhappily, this is a subject that can derail a dinner party as fast as a discussion of abortion. There are cat lovers and veterinarians who regard the declawing of cats as a standard procedure. There are other cat lovers and veterinarians who are adamantly against declawing and very passionate on the subject. And there are those who have reservations but feel it ultimately depends on the circumstances. On the following pages there are a number of specific questions on the subject. This isn't an issue that can be "settled," but there are some basic facts that can be used as a basis for judgment.

101

Serious Surgery

Q. I understand that declawing requires that a cat be given general anesthetic. *Is a general anesthetic necessary for declawing in order to keep the cat immobile, as an antidote to pain, or because the procedure is major surgery?*

A. All three factors come into play. Some veterinarians who are against the procedure warn against possible bad reactions to general anesthesia, but since these same veterinarians are willing to perform other operations under general anesthesia, this seems a moot point. Those against declawing always describe the operation in the most brutal terms, perhaps to induce squeamishness in the owner. To put it simply, the front claws are cut off at the first joint. It is important to make sure the cells that promote claw growth are removed. The paws are usually bandaged, although some veterinarians prefer to suture the paws to avoid renewed bleeding.

There is no question that the procedure requires skill, and it can be wise to have it done at an animal hospital with several vets on the staff, at least one of whom is likely to be an expert at this particular operation. There are, however, many veterinarians with solo practices who have all the experience necessary. There is nothing wrong with asking how often the veterinarian has performed the operation.

102

When to Declaw

Q. The idea of declawing is upsetting to me, but after more than a year of trying to train my cat to use a scratching post, he is still tearing up the house. *Is it harder on a cat to be declawed when it is older?*

A. Probably. Most veterinarians feel that cats adapt better when they are declawed before they are eight months old. It can even be combined with the neutering of the cat, which also of course requires general anesthesia. By the time a cat is six months old it should be clear if there is a serious clawing problem. Waiting another six months in the hope that you can train your cat to a scratching post is usually fruitless.

103

Tenderfoot

🐾

Q. My veterinarian tells me that my cat will be kept at the animal hospital for as much as three days after he is declawed. *Is it really necessary for a cat to be "hospitalized" for three days after being declawed?*

A. Although complications from declawing are not common, problems with renewed bleeding can occur. Even after returning home, a cat will often experience some tenderness for a few days. Because of the tenderness, and to avoid the possibility of any infection setting in, many veterinarians suggest that newspaper instead of cat litter be used for a few days, with the newspapers being changed two or three times a day.

104

Still Scratching Away

Q. I had my cat declawed a number of months ago. He still scratches the furniture, although of course there is no damage. *Is it normal for a cat to go on scratching after being declawed?*

A. Yes, it is completely normal. In fact it is one of the examples given by those who see no problem with declawing to support their belief that a cat suffers no long-term psychological harm from being declawed. Those who are against declawing insist that many declawed cats take to biting as a substitute for scratching. Others say this is unusual and the result of an aggressiveness that existed prior to the declawing, noting that one reason for declawing some cats is that they scratch people as well as furniture.

105

The Neutered Cat

Q. My daughter has just been given a three-month-old female kitten. We intend to have the cat neutered eventually, but I have always heard that female cats are better behaved if they are allowed to have at least one litter. *Don't female cats do better if they become a mother at least once?*

A. According to almost all the experts, this is a myth. In fact, the great majority of veterinarians say that both male and female cats make better pets if they are neutered early, no later than eight months for a female or nine months for a male. The female can be spayed as early as six months, the male castrated as early as seven months. Female cats suffer a lot when they are in heat, and males that are not able to copulate because they are kept indoors go half crazy. The advisability of having both males and females altered is indeed one of the few areas in which veterinarians are in virtually unanimous agreement. The only exception is cats that are being bred by professional breeders.

106

Neutering Costs

Q. I am a first-time cat owner. I'm about to get my female cat spayed. A friend who had her tomcat neutered said it had only cost fifty dollars, but my vet says it will be double that for my cat, plus overnight boarding. *Is the operation to neuter a female really so much more difficult that it would cost double?*

A. Yes. It's possible to castrate a male in a couple of minutes after the general anesthesia has taken hold. This is because the testicles are outside the body. Spaying a female involves making an incision in the side and removing the internal reproductive organs, and takes about fifteen minutes including the suturing.

As to boarding the cat overnight, some veterinarians insist on it but others do not. Part of the reason for keeping the cat overnight is to make sure that there are no postoperative problems. But this can usually be ascertained after a few hours. There is another reason for keeping a female cat overnight: Many owners would go into shock at seeing the dried blood on the cat, which can't very well be cleaned up entirely for twenty-four hours. If you can convince your vet that you realize your cat will be woozy and something of a mess, he may agree to let you bring her in early in the morning and pick her up at the end of the day.

107

Extra Heats

❦

Q. I did not have my cat Susannah neutered, figuring I could deal with a couple of heats a year. But she's two and a half now and she seems to be going into heat more and more often, every few weeks or so. *Is it normal for an unspayed female to have so many heats?*

A. Yes, unfortunately. An unspayed cat that does not become impregnated will have an increased number of heats until copulation finally takes place, after which she will return to a normal schedule of about five heats every two years. There is really no point in having an unspayed cat unless you are going to breed her.

108

Spraying

Q. I have a tomcat that comes and goes as he pleases, spending more than half his waking time outdoors. I had thought that since he was outdoors a lot he would not spray in the house, but he does it anyway. He's a year and a half old at this point. *Is there any point in having an adult tomcat castrated in order to cut down on spraying?*

A. Very little. The spraying of urine backward onto an object is a male cat's way of marking his territory. Even though he is outside a lot, your house is also part of that territory. Unfortunately, once a male is sexually mature, castration will not change his spraying behavior much at all. It is already part of his very being. When males are castrated as kittens, they usually do not develop the spraying habit.

109

The Caterwauling Night

Q. I grew up in the city, on the fifteenth floor of an apartment building which was quite well insulated from street noises. I recently married and moved with my husband to a college town. I have always had a cat (I'm now on my third) but they've always been indoor neutered cats. In the town I now live in there are lots of cats roaming around. They seem to have homes, but at certain times of the year, when the females are in heat, the racket that goes on in the middle of the night is startling. I now understand the meaning of the word "caterwauling." I've gotten used to it all, but I am curious. *Why do mating cats sound like they're having a barroom brawl?*

A. Because in a sense they are. There is no doubt a tomcat regards the area around your house as part of his territory. He will regard any female cat in heat that shows up in that territory as rightfully his. But males with adjacent territories will inevitably be attracted by the calls and scent of the female. Most of what you hear—and it can go on for days—are sounds of aggression, brawling if you will, as the males compete for the right to mate with the female.

At intervals, as the days go by, you will hear a different sound, a kind of high-pitched scream. This is the female reacting to the withdrawal of the penis following copulation, which lasts only seconds. It is a cry of pain, not pleasure. The tomcat's penis has spines on it that point downward toward the base. These spines rake the vagina during withdrawal. There is some debate about the exact process, but it is generally agreed that the raking of the vagina is crucial to ovulation in the female. Ovulation does not take place for as long as twenty-four hours afterward, and for pregnancy to be assured, repeated copulation is required after ovulation has begun. The females have much more sexual stamina than the males, which is why a litter may have kittens with more than one father; as one male loses interest, another will take over. And eventually the heat will end and the noise subside.

110

Giving Birth Is Not a Performance Art

Q. Our cat is about to have her first litter. My children, who are seven and nine, are very excited and want to be sure we wake them up if the cat starts to give birth in the middle of the night. I have no objection to my children watching, but I wonder if it's good for the cat. *How much privacy does a cat need while giving birth?*

A. As much as possible. I assume you have provided your cat with a nesting place. Many experts, stressing the privacy issue, suggest that the birthing nest should be a cardboard box with a lid on it and a hole cut in the side. The box should be lined with newspaper and placed somewhere out of the way. Some cats prefer to create their own nesting places; don't interfere if that's the case.

As to your kids watching, let them sleep, and if it happens during the day, keep them at some distance and tell them not to make *any* noise. Nervous or excited human beings make the mother nervous and complicate her job. A cat that has had several litters may become relatively blasé about the event, and onlookers will be less disturbing.

There are, it should be said, some cats that insist upon having their owners present when they give birth. But these dependent creatures are exceptions. If your cat does invite you to be present, by all means accept.

111

The Favored Nipple

Q. Our cat recently had kittens. (All had good homes arranged for them in advance.) During the first few weeks, I noticed something interesting about the way the kittens suckled. For about the first two weeks, each kitten always used the same nipple. But then suddenly they began changing from one nipple to another at each feeding. *Why do kittens stick to one nipple at first and then start changing the pattern?*

A. The kittens are initially pushed into place at a given nipple by the mother. Since they are both blind and deaf for the first two weeks of their lives, the kittens have to rely chiefly on their sense of smell, and thus return to the nipple already imprinted with their own particular scent. But once they can see, they express their newfound curiosity by exploring the mother's other nipples.

112

Nursing Hunger

Q. While she was nursing her first litter, our cat seemed to be perpetually hungry. We kept putting out more and more food, and she kept gobbling it up. *Is it good for a cat to give her large quantities of food while she is nursing?*

A. During lactation, cats need all the food they can get. They are dispensing much more milk in relation to their body weight than is true of human beings. Keep putting fresh food out and let the cat decide how much to eat—her body is giving her excellent instructions.

113

The Rejected Kitten

Q. Our cat had a litter of six kittens. At some point she apparently carried one of them into another room and left it there. It was still wet so we dried it off and returned it to the nest. A few minutes later our cat ate the kitten. I knew enough not to try to stop it, but I'm still having a hard time dealing with it. *Why would a mother cat eat a kitten?*

A. We really don't know, but it is not uncommon. Some cats seem to have a problem at the moment of birth and eat the kitten along with the umbilical cord. This may simply be accidental. But if a mother cat rejects a kitten and removes it from the nest, it means that that kitten is not wanted, whatever the reason may be. In fact, you were lucky. When a rejected kitten is returned to the nest, the mother sometimes turns on and devours the entire litter. A rejected kitten, most veterinarians advise, should be allowed to die, cruel as that may seem. It is extremely difficult to keep a kitten alive that has been rejected by its mother; trying to do so is often just delaying the inevitable.

114

The Adoptable Stray

Q. It seems to me that I see stray cats everywhere I go. I feel so sorry for them, but I've been told that trying to rescue a stray is a very iffy proposition. *How difficult is it to success-fully adopt a stray cat?*

A. Various organizations have come up with different figures on how many homeless cats there are in the United States. But whether it is a matter of a dozen stray cats for every one with a home or some twenty million additional stray cats a year, the numbers are huge. Very few stray cats survive more than a year or so, but of course they produce millions of new homeless kittens in that time.

Adopting a stray cat is thus making only a very small dent in a very large problem. Moreover, the difficulties in dealing with a stray cat are numerous. Any stray cat is likely to have a slew of medical problems and it can cost hundreds of dollars to return it to health. Beyond that, most strays have lost their sense of trust in human beings and restoring that bond requires great patience. There are people who can cope with the problems, but unless you are willing to spend a lot of money and time, it's not advisable to try to rescue a stray you happen to see wandering around in an area any distance from your home. And you probably should not attempt it if you have a cat or cats already. The stray will have to be kept separated from your own pets until it is healthy, and even then it may be impossible to integrate the stray into the existing pet family—strays have grown used to fighting other cats in order to survive.

The exception to this generally bleak picture is a cat that decides to adopt you—hanging around your doorstep or backyard and imploring to be cared for. To begin with, this behavior means that the cat has not been a stray for long and still looks to human beings for care. You have a head start. Even in this situation, count on several trips to the veterinarian and recognize that this wanderer may have to remain an outside cat, especially if you have other indoor cats. I know many people who have such outdoor cats that they have cared for; they are never surprised, however, if the cat ultimately disappears again.

115

The Well-Preserved Cat

Q. When I tell people that my cat is nineteen years old, they often do not believe me. The idea seems to be that the average life span of a cat is about twelve years, and that fifteen years is extraordinary and nineteen years absurd. I'm even accused of lying about my cat's age for effect. *How old can cats live to be?*

A. Cats begin to enter old age at nine years, and the "average" life expectancy is eleven to thirteen years, depending on whose statistics you want to believe. But there are a surprising number of cats that survive into their late teens, and some even reach the age of twenty-five. Such cats have in essence spent the majority of their lives in old age. But even senile cats function better than senile dogs.

Obviously, cats that live to a great age have "good genes," but they have almost always been exceptionally well cared for. In particular, that means that they have been taken to the vet on a regular basis, not just when a crisis arrives. Veterinarians routinely report that more than two thirds of the animals they see are dogs, despite the fact that the pet cat population now exceeds the pet dog population. Someone who has a very old cat has clearly cared enough to take very special care of it.

116

An Old-Age Companion?

🐾

Q. My cat Louisa May is almost fourteen. Her appetite is still fine but she has slowed down a lot and obviously has some arthritis. I was thinking about getting a kitten as a companion for her. My neighbor, who has an old beagle named Sam, got a puppy and Sam seems to have gotten a new lease on life. *Is it a good idea to get a kitten to keep an old cat company?*

A. No. The presence of a puppy can indeed rejuvenate an old dog in many cases, at least temporarily, but it doesn't work the same way with cats, for several reasons. First, you must remember that dogs are social animals and cats are not. Dogs relate to one another in a much more fulsome way than cats do. Second, old cats get very set in their ways, and the last thing they want is to have their routine turned upside down. Beyond that, Louisa May is likely to resent the competition for your affection.

117

A Sad End

Q. My mother recently died, leaving a ten-year-old cat named Doris. My mother lived near us, and I am fond of Doris myself, but I cannot possibly have her live with us since we have two dogs that would as soon jump a cat as look at one. It might be that Doris could inflict more harm than would be visited on her, but I can't have that either. I've tried to find someone else to take Doris, without success. *What are the possibilities of a ten-year-old cat getting adopted if I send her to an animal shelter?*

A. Practically nil. It's almost certain that Doris would be put to sleep in a few days—shelters have vastly more cats thrust upon them than they can possibly find homes for. In the meantime, poor Doris will be miserably unhappy in her cage in strange and very unsettling surroundings. If you cannot find anyone to take her—and a ten-year-old cat is going to have a hard time adjusting to even a nice new home—it is probably best to have her put to sleep by a veterinarian. Decisions like these are difficult and sad, but if she's going to be put to sleep anyway, taking her to her regular veterinarian is the most humane way to deal with it. Some people have such a hard time facing this problem that they put cats out of the car in a nice neighborhood and hope the cat will find a home itself. That is truly cruel.

118

The Cat Across the Hall

Q. I live in a smallish apartment building in New York. The man who lives across the hall from me is a musician. He's a very pleasant sort, and I allowed myself to be roped into feeding his cat when he's out of town. This happens about every couple of months, and he's usually gone for a week, entertaining on a cruise ship. I don't mind feeding the cat, but what worries me is that I never see it. The food is always gone, but the cat apparently hides the minute it hears me turning the key. I've stayed around for as much as half an hour trying to coax it out, but with no success. The owner says not to worry, the cat is just like that, but I wonder if the cat isn't awfully unhappy. *Is a cat that's left alone so much, with just a neighbor to feed it, being mistreated?*

A. I wouldn't say that mistreated is the right word, but certainly it isn't having a very happy time of it. On the other hand, it would probably be even more miserable if it were boarded. I once found myself in a similar situation. I had just returned from four years of living in Europe and didn't have a cat of my own yet. The neighbor across the hall was a singer, with a similar traveling situation. I offered to take the cat into my apartment, but the owner said it would be happier where it was, which was probably true. I finally did make friends with the cat and she would come out and play, but it took months. One thing that reassured me was that whenever the singer came home, the cat greeted him with ecstasy. I once listened at the door for a bit, and the singer was telling the cat the entire story of his trip. He was still at it when I went out an hour later!

147

119

Moving Daze

🐾

Q. My husband works for a company that tends to move its employees around the country a lot as they are promoted. We have a six-year-old son who is driving us crazy about getting him a pet. A cat seems more sensible to me than a dog, because it is small and easy to carry. But my husband says dogs adjust better to new locations. *Do cats really become very unhappy when they move to a new home?*

A. Cats are far more territorial than dogs. As a result, many cats get extremely upset when they are moved, especially if it happens often. There are many stories of cats that have simply disappeared because they did not like their new surroundings. If you have an outdoor cat, it is going to get into fights in the new location before being accepted in to the local hierarchy of outdoor cats. Anyone who has an outdoor cat and is moving should make sure to contact a veterinarian first thing on arrival in the new town, because it is very likely you will need one to patch up your cat. A cat, especially a male, who's a stranger in town is in a sense "looking for trouble."

Indoor cats, on the other hand, know virtually nothing but their homes. Thus it can be quite traumatic to be introduced to entirely new surroundings, especially on a continuing basis. A cat is not going to get used to moving—it is going to get increasingly upset. In terms of your life-style, your husband is right. Get a dog, a toy breed if you're worried about size. Dogs are far more adaptable to new surroundings.

120

How About a Valium?

Q. I am going to be flying from Philadelphia to the West Coast shortly to house-sit for friends who are taking a round-the-world cruise. I'm taking my cat with me. She hates even traveling by car. A friend says she gives her cat a very small amount of Valium when she travels by air and that it works wonderfully. *Is it safe to give a cat a human drug like Valium?*

A. A lot of people do this with dogs, but cats are so small that it's taking a chance on a bad reaction. With any pet, it seems wisest to use a tranquilizer that is specifically prescribed by your vet in a very exact dosage.

121

Miraculous Journeys

Q. My sister and her husband lost their cat six months ago during a month-long summer vacation in the mountains about four hundred miles from where they live. Now a cat has turned up on their doorstep that they are convinced is their long-lost pet, although I'm not sure how they could tell since their cat was a very miscellaneous-looking marmalade. I'm happy they have a new pet but dubious it's the same one. *Can a cat really find its way home over a four-hundred-mile stretch of country?*

A. There are many stories of this happening, but very few of them have been thoroughly verified. In most cases a near look-alike turns up and is immediately accepted as the missing pet. But there are a few indisputable cases that involve cats finding their way home—or back to the home they lived in before the family moved, having disliked the new house and decamped.

There are numerous theories about how a cat could make such a trek successfully, ranging from the psychic to the at least potentially scientific. The most plausible I've come across concerns the ability of some animals—birds in particular—to find their way because they have an internal clock that differentiates between the light where they are and the light where they used to be. Maybe, but one has to wonder about the passing seasons when it takes the cat months to make the journey. If a cat can really calculate all the variables it is wondrous indeed.

122

The Best-Bet Vet

*:

Q. I'm moving to a rather spread-out city in another state where I understand there are two or three dozen veterinarians to choose from. *Is the best way to find a new vet to simply ask neighbors and co-workers?*

A. That's a step up from just choosing the nearest one listed in the yellow pages. But be sure to ask several people and keep in mind that your co-worker Suzie Q may like a certain vet for his winning smile as much as for any expertise, while your neighbor may warn you away from the best vet in town simply because he refused to take the vet's advice and lost a pet. If you get two or more people making the same recommendation, give the vet a try. Beyond that, it becomes as personal a decision as choosing a physician for yourself—apply the same criteria.

There is one clue that almost never applies to physicians anymore—does a vet give out his home phone number to steady customers? There are still vets that actually do this, and it is a strong indication of caring. The vet probably won't give you the number right away. He or she will want to see if you bring your pet in for regular examinations and booster shots before making that extra commitment to you. But the vet who does give a home phone number to at least some of his clients is usually a good bet.

123

Keeping the Dander Down

🐾

Q. To my horror I have just discovered that my husband-to-be is apparently allergic to cats. (We met in Europe, where I was working for two years, and I had left my cat with my parents, so his problem came as a late surprise.) I've always had cats and I hate to think of going through the rest of my life without one. *Exactly what causes people to be allergic to cats, and do very shorthaired cats create less of a problem?*

A. An allergic reaction to cats is usually caused by what is called "dander," a mixture of hair, cat saliva, and flaking skin. Children are more often allergic, and often outgrow the condition, but an adult who is prone to hay fever may have a genuine problem. Shorthaired cats don't seem to lessen the reaction all that much. There is a hairless cat, a mutation that is called the sphinx, but only a very few stalwarts have bred the sphinx since it looks more like a miniature dog and is not popular. But there is a possible solution, another mutation known as the rex. The rex has very tightly curled, extremely soft fur, and is increasing considerably in popularity, not least because it seems to produce very little dander. There is a Devon rex and a Cornish rex, as well as a German mutation, but only experts can tell them apart.

124

The Medicinal Cat

Q. When I come home from a tough day, the first thing I do is sit down and take my cat Belinda in my lap and stroke her. This isn't just because she seems glad to see me or that I'm trying to make up for leaving her alone all day. It also makes me feel calmer and more refreshed. *Is it true that stroking my cat may actually help to lower my blood pressure?*

A. Yes, the evidence is quite strong on this point. It doesn't work for everyone, of course. The blood pressure of someone who dislikes cats will go up even when that person is merely in the same room with one. So the question remains whether it is the cat itself or an individual's feeling about the cat that causes the change in blood pressure.

There are also new studies that suggest that having a pet—a cat, a dog, or even a bird—increases human longevity. Pets have also been found to have therapeutic value in nursing homes and for people, especially children, recovering from serious illnesses or injuries. Because they are small and demand less care and attention than dogs, cats appear to be especially useful in this regard.

125

Who's in Charge Here?

Q. I have had many cats over the years, and all of them have liked to climb up into my lap to be petted or played with. Some liked to do this more than others, but even those who seemed to like it best always seemed to decide, very suddenly, that they had had enough. *Is the way cats suddenly stop playing and go off to do something else just a matter of their vaunted independence or is there something more to it?*

A. This question has always been asked about cats and no doubt always will be. There is a school of thought among cat experts that the cat was not really domesticated by human beings but rather decided that attaching itself to human households was a pretty good deal, making life quite a lot easier. Proponents of this theory believe that cats wandered into the human picture, were found useful as ratcatchers and rewarded with additional food, and simply decided to stick around. In this view, despite having become more dependent on human beings over the millennia, cats still retain a "look, I've just dropped in, see ya" attitude that serves to remind us of their underlying wild natures.

Perhaps the great French philosopher Montaigne put it best: "When I play with my cat, who knows whether she isn't amusing herself with me more than I am with her."

Bibliography

Beadle, Muriel. *The Cat*. New York: Simon & Schuster, Inc., 1977.
Boorer, Michael. *Wild Cats*. New York: Grosset & Dunlap, Inc., 1970.
Caras, Roger A. *A Celebration of Cats*. New York: Simon & Schuster, Inc., 1986.
———. *A Cat Is Watching*. New York: Simon & Schuster, Inc., 1989.
Carlson, Delbert G., and James M. Griffin. *Cat Owner's Home Veterinary Handbook*. New York: Howell, 1983.
Corey, Paul. *Do Cats Think?* Secaucus, N.J.: Castle, 1977.
Dale-Green, Patricia. *The Cult of the Cat*. London: William Heinemann Co., 1963.
Drimmer, Frederick, ed. *The Animal Kingdom*. New York: Greystone Press, 1954.
Fireman, Judy, ed. *Cat Catalogue*. New York: Workman Publishing Co., 1976.
Fox, Michael W. *Understanding Your Cat*. New York: Coward, McCann & Geoghegan, Inc., 1974.
Kritsick, Stephen M. *Cat Care*. New York: Simon & Schuster, 1986.
Lessing, Doris. *Particularly Cats*. New York: New American Library, 1971.
Loeb, Jo, and Paul Loeb. *You Can Train Your Cat*. Feltham, Eng.: Hamlyn Publishing Group, Ltd., 1977.
McGinnis, Terri. *The Well Cat Book*. New York: Random House, 1975.
McNulty, Faith, and Elisabeth Keiffer. *Wholly Cats*. New York: Gramercy Publishing Company, 1962.
Méry, Fernand. *The Life, History and Magic of the Cat*. New York: Grosset & Dunlap, Inc., 1968.
Morris, Desmond. *Catwatching*. New York: Crown Publishers, Inc., 1987.
Necker, Claire. *The Natural History of Cats*. New York: A. S. Barnes and Co., 1970.
Pond, Grace, ed. *The Complete Cat Encyclopedia*. New York: Arco, 1975.

Riddle, Roz. *The City Cat.* New York: Charles Scribner's Sons, 1984.
Ritvo, Harriet. *The Animal Estate.* Cambridge, Mass.: Harvard University Press, 1987.
Siller, Frederick Cameron, and Ruth Mary Meyler. *Cats Ancient and Modern.* New York: Viking Press, 1966.
Wood, Gerald. *Animal Facts and Feats.* Garden City, N.Y.: Doubleday & Co., Inc., 1972.
Wright, Michael, and Sally Waltus, eds. *The Book of the Cat.* New York: Summit Books, 1980.

INDEX

157

158

159

puppies, 45, 145
purebred cats, 21, 28, 31, 32, 33, 34, 42
purring, 54, 55

rabies, 47
rats, 19, 108–109
red points, 43
REM (rapid eye movement) sleep, 65
respiratory viruses, 47
rex mutation, 152
Rhine, J. B., 62
rhinotracheitis, 47
Riddle, Roz, 42
"rumpies," 33
Russian blue cats, 37, 94

scratching posts, 124–125, 126, 129
seal points, 28
sex, choosing cat by, 41
Shakespeare, William, 103
shorthair cats:
    American, 23, 28, 34, 39, 85
    British, 34
Siamese cats, 15, 23, 28, 29, 30, 34, 35, 36, 39, 43, 48, 55, 88
size, 39
sneering, 57
socialization, 16–17, 39, 46, 58, 95
spaying, 132, 134
Spectrum A colors, 28
Spectrum B colors, 28
speed, 86
sphinx cats, 152
spraying, 135
sterility, 40
strays, 87, 142–143

"stumpies," 33
superstition, 20

tabby cats, 28, 29
tails:
    absence of, 33
    kinky, 36
    movement of, 56, 58
tapetum lucidem, 69
temperature, 77–78, 120
Tennyson, Alfred, Lord, 38
toes, extra, 37
tongues, 73
tortoiseshell cats, 28, 31, 40
tranquilizers, 149
travel, 148–149
trees, 76, 86
tricks, 90
Turkish angora cats, 23

urinary blockage, 112, 122
urination, 80, 122, 135

vaccinations, 47
Valium, 149
vegetarianism, 106
veterinarians, 47, 84, 100–101, 104, 112, 120, 127, 128, 129, 132, 133, 146, 148, 151
vibrissae, 53
vocal sounds, 39, 43, 55, 136–137

weather, predicting of, 63
Weir, Harrison, 22
whiskers, 52–53, 70
wild cats, 14, 16, 79, 92, 113
Williams, Tennessee, 77
witches, 18, 20